# Children and Youth in Africa

# Children and Youth in Africa
## Annotated Bibliography
## 2001–2011

Mwenda Ntarangwi

**CODESRIA**

Council for the Development of Social Science Research in Africa
DAKAR

© CODESRIA 2014
Council for the Development of Social Science Research in Africa
Avenue Cheikh Anta Diop, Angle Canal IV
BP 3304 Dakar, 18524, Senegal
Website: www.codesria.org

ISBN: 978-2-86978-587-8

Typesetter: Sériane Camara Ajavon
Cover Design: Ibrahima Fofana

Distributed in Africa by CODESRIA

Distributed elsewhere by African Books Collective, Oxford, UK.
Website: www.africanbookscollective.com

The Council for the Development of Social Science Research in Africa (CODESRIA) is an independent organisation whose principal objectives are to facilitate research, promote research-based publishing and create multiple forums geared towards the exchange of views and information among African researchers. All these are aimed at reducing the fragmentation of research in the continent through the creation of thematic research networks that cut across linguistic and regional boundaries.

CODESRIA publishes *Africa Development*, the longest standing Africa based social science journal; *Afrika Zamani*, a journal of history; the *African Sociological Review*; the *African Journal of International Affairs*; *Africa Review of Books* and the *Journal of Higher Education in Africa*. The Council also co-publishes the *Africa Media Review*; *Identity, Culture and Politics: An Afro-Asian Dialogue*; *The African Anthropologist* and the *Afro-Arab Selections for Social Sciences*. The results of its research and other activities are also disseminated through its Working Paper Series, Green Book Series, Monograph Series, Book Series, Policy Briefs and the CODESRIA Bulletin. Select CODESRIA publications are also accessible online at www.codesria.org.

CODESRIA would like to express its gratitude to the Swedish International Development Cooperation Agency (SIDA/SAREC), the International Development Research Centre (IDRC), the Ford Foundation, the MacArthur Foundation, the Carnegie Corporation, the Norwegian Agency for Development Cooperation (NORAD), the Danish Agency for International Development (DANIDA), the French Ministry of Cooperation, the United Nations Development Programme (UNDP), the Netherlands Ministry of Foreign Affairs, the Rockefeller Foundation, FINIDA, the Canadian International Development Agency (CIDA), the Open Society Foundations (OSFs), TrustAfrica, UN/UNICEF, the African Capacity Building Foundation (ACBF) and the Government of Senegal for supporting its research, training and publication programmes.

# Contents

# Introduction

This annotated bibliography provides a summary of scholarly work specifically focused on children and youth in Africa published between 2001 and 2011 in both journals and books. This project is commissioned and sponsored by the Council for the Development of Social Science Research in Africa (CODESRIA). As the leading social science research organisation in Africa, CODESRIA has for decades pursued the study and scholarship of youth and children, especially through its Child and Youth Studies Programme. The Programme's main objective, among others, is to strengthen research capacity in the fields of child and youth studies across linguistic and disciplinary boundaries in Africa.

In 2003 CODESRIA published a monograph titled 'Annotated Bibliography on Childhood with Emphasis on Africa: Outline, General Findings and Research Recommendations' written by Dr. Patti Henderson. That publication presents the major works from anthropological, sociological and psychological literatures pertaining to child studies, extracts from the political sciences and economics, and key theoretical texts from other parts of the world. In this current bibliography a similar approach is undertaken to capture the subsequent works of the ensuing ten years but exclusively limited to titles focusing on Africa and also without foregrounding any particular publications. Henderson's theoretical analysis on the study of children and youth in Africa emphasized the disconnect between, on the one hand, the ways in which adults think about and construct children and their lives, and on the other, how children actually experience and live their lives. This has led to the perception of children as 'in need of protection and as occupying a transitional social space on the road to adulthood'.[1]

While some African scholars have questioned this view of children especially when it comes to their own agency and full participation in socioeconomic production for households,[2] the idea of children as vulnerable social subjects continues to shape much of the research that was carried out on African children in the period covered in this monograph. This view of children as passive and vulnerable is also reflected in much of the work and perceptions of children in the West especially when seen from an economic perspective. Western restrictions on specific age limits that govern children's participation in work or labour, whether paid or not, and the subsequent rights that go along with them are often not easily translatable to many African contexts. As is often in the case of children acting as household heads and fending not only for themselves but for their siblings and times their parents, the Western notion of children as 'emotionally priceless but economically useless'[3] is not tenable. This construction of African children and youth in terms of received Western categories of personhood is still very strong today.

The overwhelming focus of research publications on HIV/AIDS and orphans, violence and child-soldiers, children's rights, and street children, demonstrates this continued interest in regarding children as vulnerable and in need of adult protection. Moreover, with most of the research projects being shaped by external funding agencies it is not surprising that many of the research questions being pursued tend to focus on areas of study preferred by these agencies. Focusing on the vulnerable child in Africa is mostly a result of the construction of childhood in modern (mostly) Western perception of childhood based on chronological age. As Boyden and Berry have argued, when challenging the overuse of trauma in analyzing the effect of war on children and youth, 'age is not necessarily the critical determinant of vulnerability'.[4] There are indications, that this research by Boyden and Berry is part of a body of literature that is challenging this notion of children as vulnerable and instead presenting them as active and independently-thinking agents of their own lives. New scholarship, especially that which focuses on popular culture, shows that youth are not only very creative and at times keen on reproducing traditions that are currently being challenged by global forces, but are also reshaping politics and the use of public urban spaces for the benefit of the larger population. These kinds of studies and scholarship help build an image of African children that not only challenges certain constructions of their identity and experiences but also provides an opportunity for their entry into public discourse through self-representation. Another way to show the complexity of the lives of African children and youth is to broaden the research methods themselves. This is a topic I now turn to in the next section.

## The Future of Research on Children and Youth in Africa

Research on youth and children in Africa as I have shown has some challenges especially because of the politics of power inequalities between those shaping research and those being studied. These inequalities lead to research framing based more on a desire to have a globalized definition of childhood and a focus on specific topics than on the realities of lived experiences of children and youth in multiple African contexts. I want to argue that there are two key research approaches that will shape the future of research on children and youth in Africa in the coming decades. The first one is what I would term as an afrocentric framing of research questions and practices regarding not only how children and youth are defined and understood but also how questions about how best to understand and write about them will emerge. The second one is an in depth qualitative research that allows for a more nuanced understanding of social realities that are lived out and expressed by African children and youth. There is some good movement within existing literature towards these two critical areas but there is a lot of room for more. Let me expand on these two research approaches as they pertain to work carried out on/with/by children and youth in Africa.

One important voice in the study of childhood in Africa is Bame Nsamenang, a Cameroonian psychologist whose writing is hinged on the premise that all knowledge is subjective and the preponderance of Western-derived theories and research practices being applied uncritically in Africa will lead to confusion that will produce no valuable evidence of how to respond to Africa's issues pertaining to children and youth today.[5] In his critique of Euro-American views on human development and intelligence, for instance, Nsamenang argues that such views have been presented as applicable to all human diversity even though they greatly differ with an African worldview. He shows that in an African worldview, knowledge is not 'separated into discrete disciplines but interwoven into a common tapestry . . . learned in a participatory curriculum'.[6] This important critique of what has come to be considered a universal view of

3

childhood supported by funding agencies emanating from the west and mobilized through research carried out by Western researchers independently or with local interlocutors who do not have much power to define the terms of research, should shape the future of research on children and youth in Africa. Indeed, Western notions of development that are 'child-centered and individualistic in nature', differs with those within an African worldview where 'a sense of self cannot be achieved without reference to the community of other humans in terms of being interconnected and enacting one's social roles'.[7]

Work by Jagwe in central Uganda on the impact of a children's rights awareness campaign reveals this need for a contextualized Afrocentric approach to any programming meant for the good of an African community. In the case study presented by Jagwe parents involved in the project 'appreciated the campaign for reminding them of what they needed to do to ensure proper development but detested the way the campaign was launched without appropriate consultations with the adult community'.[8] As a result of starting the rights education process with school children because of the individualized sense of personhood prevalent in the western cultures the funding for the program came from, made parents totally opposed to the rights themselves because their children 'became 'rebellious' and undermined their parents' authority by directly reporting them to authorities'.[9] Ethnographic research even in the US around issues of early childhood education underscores the value of understanding and mobilizing children's cultural identities, relationships, and understandings of learning contexts for programs to be successful in meeting children's learning needs.[10] How then can an understanding of African children and youth lives be exempt from such contextualization and application of local knowledge systems and ways of responding to immediate environments? Thankfully the work of Nsamenang as well as that of Kofi Marfo are continually providing this Afrocentric approach to understanding African children and youth by providing practical examples of how scholars in and outside Africa are and can utilize such an approach to better represent their research constituencies. Two recent texts edited by Bame Nsamenang and Therese Tchombe and by Auma Okwany, Elizabeth Ngutuku, and Arthur Muchangi are important contributions to this field.[11] An Afrocentric framing of research and practice regarding studies of children and youth in Africa starts on the premise that contextualization and appreciation of African local knowledge and lived realities are critical and that Western models of studying and carrying out research in Africa have to be critically assessed and reframed if they are be applied usefully in the African context. Such an understanding as I argue below is best accessed through ethnographic or qualitative research.

Currently most research on children and youth in Africa seems to be limited by the lack of sustained ethnographic research that would capture trends, indeterminacy, innovation, and fluidity experienced individually or communally. Given the enormity of Africa as a geographic and cultural region as well as the diversity of social and political experiences, preferred research methods such as surveys and questionnaires will not yield information that is useful in understanding the critical issues affecting African children and youth. I argue that what studies of African children and youth need is ethnographic research that analyses what anthropologists call 'thick descriptions' that provide thick descriptions that will help us chip away at the assumed universal experiences and understandings of children and youth prevalent in the literature today.

Ethnography by anthropologists in numerous African countries, for instance, has complicated some of the assumptions made by scholars about human cultural practices and experiences. Let me share some examples. For a long time psychologists had assumed universal prescriptions of what is termed 'mother-infant attachment' in which using praises or interrogatives when addressing their children as well as looking at and talking to them promote healthy emotional and psychosocial growth. Research in Kenya by Robert Levine carried out over two decades showed that Gusii parents would have fitted the category of 'weak attachment' between mothers and children (identified by psychologists) because the mothers would ignore their children's vocalizations such as babbling and even used commands and threats on them instead of the expected quick and 'polite' responses. Levine found no emotional crippling to the children as they grew up into young adults.[12] Another assumption about social reality mobilized by researchers for a long time is the notion of the 'life course' where individuals are said to move progressively from one stage of life to another such as from childhood to adulthood or motherhood. Jennifer Johnson-Hanks' research among Beti women of Southern Cameroon shows that motherhood does not place young women into adulthood because motherhood as a loosely bounded fluid status allows them to move in and out of social categories depending on their ability to earn their 'personhood'.[13] This idea of an earned adulthood is not new in other African communities as shown by Kristen Cheney in her work in Uganda where she argues that adult social status in Africa is achieved 'much more so than in Western culture, where the age of majority is reinforced by law'.[14]

In their review of literature on youth and war, Boyden and Berry state that, 'the accepted wisdom is that, the impact (of war on children) is resoundingly negative and seen as consistent since it is generally thought that child development and wellbeing are based on biological and psychological structures that are fairly uniform across class and culture'.[15] Indeed, this universalized expectation of the impact that war has on children has led to the use of precoded research tools that end up reproducing very specific and similar results coded under such terms as trauma, victims and perpetrators as well as results fitting the assumed psychological, emotional, and physical effects of war. As Boyden and Berry go on to show, this focus on psychological assessments on individuals ignores 'massive societal transformations that pervade all aspects of society, its institutions, political structures, cultures, economy, and communication systems'.[16]

Insights into these complex sociocultural realities that challenge assumed universal human experiences cannot be obtained through the now prevalent short term qualitative precoded research tools. Research that applies surveys through questionnaires can avail to the researcher a cheap and quick way of gathering data from large numbers of study populations because with closed and restricted questions one can generate statistical summaries that lead to broad generalizations. When administered correctly questionnaires can be a valuable research tool for providing not only representative information about a very large group but also measure certain trends in a population. Questionnaires and surveys can, however, be problematic when administered in a research project in which the data sought requires observation and context analysis as is the case with many of the research areas highlighted in this monograph. Behavior change analysis among street children, youth at risk of sexually transmittable infections, rehabilitated combat veterans, all need a much deeper understanding that cannot be gleaned from surveys and questionnaires. Such topics need a more indepth analysis that is best accessed through qualitative research that uses fieldwork.

Fieldwork helps a researcher establish facts about people or places as well as establish validity and accuracy of existing data. People's attitudes may be established through surveys mailed to respondents but a keen researcher will know that attitudes may not entirely be measured or recorded by answering structured questions. Attitudes may be reflected in people's interaction with their environment or other people, non-verbal communication, or in discursive practices, all of which cannot be adequately recorded through a structured questionnaire. I am not oblivious to the research realities attendant in Africa especially as it pertains to children and youth. Research funds are limited and when available such funds are mostly disbursed by external funding agencies with their own research priorities. Many a time research in Africa also is carried out through consultancies but this does not mean that the researchers themselves cannot shape the overall research practice itself. As Ntarangwi, Mills and Babiker have argued, even consultancies can lead to long term qualitative projects when researchers build on and feed off of research carried out in the same geographic location by different consultants.[17] It only takes some level of awareness and sharing of what has been done before in the same location to establish a rich data set of a phenomenon or community that can allow for a longitudinal and/or deeper understanding of phenomena or community. Repeated consultancies in the same community as is often the case in many parts of Africa, can lead to an accumulated data that over time can produce a rich ethnography.

## Trends in Research on Children and Youth in Africa Between 2001-2011

As I have mentioned above there is a preponderance of research on specific topics on children and youth that focus on the theme of vulnerability or deviance because of the existing constructions of Africa and its people as well as due to sources of and priorities for funding to carry out such research. This means that there are a few areas of research that require more concerted effort as they seem quite neglected by the literature covered in this monograph even though they are important in providing a holistic view of the lives and experiences of children and youth in contemporary Africa. Studies of disabilities, parents' relationships (especially fathers) with their children, children's and youth beliefs and spirituality, and the specific social powers wielded by children and youth, are examples of such topics. These research areas as shown in this monograph all require increased attention and support because they are critical to a broader reflection of the continuous changes African societies are going through. Unfortunately they may not be in line with some of the major research programs supported by external funding agencies that have been central in growing African scholarship and research on children and youth. That notwithstanding African scholars have a duty to carry out such research for the sake of their societies. I will now focus on the sub-topics of research written between 2001 and 2011 focusing on children and youth in Africa. In choosing to organize these topics into the categories provided, I am hoping to show the more established categories of research such as orphans and child headed households while also inviting some new ways of looking at children and youth experiences under such topics as power shifts and media representation which allow us different angles of thinking about children and youth in Africa.

## Child/Youth Agency and Perceptions/Reflections

Much of the research carried out in Africa on children and youth has tended to treat them as passive entities whose ideas and activities are best articulated by researchers or caregivers responding on their behalf. As a demographically young continent, however, Africa is seeing a great shift in the ways children and youth experience their lives and even relate to adults. In this section I highlight works that not only show how this population perceives themselves and their world but also the shifting power relations between youth and adults especially as they continue to have more access to knowledge of the world availed through new media. How do youth renegotiate and even reconfigure social life in opposition to expected normative behaviour mobilized by local lore and social expectations? What are the experiences and even aspirations of children regarding their lives and their future? Some of the works included here address these and other related issues but it is an area that needs more input. Let me highlight just one such project.

The practice of denying children and youth in Africa voice and agency when presenting their perceptions and experiences of their lives was challenged through a eight country project initiated by the UNICEF Eastern and Southern Africa Regional office and the African Child Policy Forum in 2006. Through research carried out among five hundred (500) children and youth in each of the eight countries (Angola, Botswana, Burundi, Ethiopia, Malawi, Rwanda, Somalia, and Tanzania) it became clear that children and youth in Africa not only have specific insights and interpretations of their lived experiences but also have crucial information and opinions about how policies and advocacy affecting them ought to be developed and implemented. When asked about the best ways of solving a problem, about 53 per cent of respondents in Angola felt that talking to each other was preferable to screaming or hitting each other, which they ranked as 2 per cent and 0 per cent respectively. When asked the same question, 93 per cent of respondents from Malawi favored talking to each other compared to 3 per cent that favored screaming at each other. Such an approach to understanding the opinions of children and youth holds promise for the critical role they play in shaping their current and future lives. Making African children and youth central participants in expressing and interpreting their lives is a positive step for Africa's survival. In the scholarly works placed under this section, I highlight these reports as well as other works that have approached children and youth as active agents in their lives, showing them as actively involved in reflecting on their own lives and making calculated decisions about themselves and the future.

## Child Labour and Child-Headed Households

What constitutes child labour and how old should children be before they are able to hold gainful employment? Do children have adequate emotional energy to make decisions about gainful work? Should children be protected from work even when such work is the only source of income for their families? What about children who are themselves heads of households, should they not work for the survival of siblings left under their care as well as for their own survival? What about children living in urban areas where there is no immediate adult supervision as in the case of street children? These and other related questions continue to occupy the minds of scholars and activists alike as well as pages of many scholarly papers and books. Child labour and child-headed households are important topics in Africa today as they were in the last few decades and a number of scholars have researched and discussed them variably. The philosophical, sociological, and even economic explanations and definitions of childhood and labour undergird many of the discussions many scholars have on these issues as shown in the selections made for this monograph. The social construction of childhood is now an accepted phenomenon in much of the scholarship on African social realities and the idea of child labour is very much tied to such constructions. As sociologist Victor Muzvidziwa has argued there needs to be a differentiation between child labour and child work stating that in many poor African communities children have to work for their own survival as well as for their households.[18]

To criminalize all work undertaken by children especially using the realm of child labour or rights fails to address the politics and realities of survival faced by such children. That said, however, we have to differentiate between work carried out in relatively 'safe' contexts and that carried out in dangerous zones such as in mines, in war zones, or in construction where the risk of injury is increased by the children's inexperience and general vulnerability. Papers and books in this section address various issues tied to work and other socioeconomic activities that children and youth are involved in showing that as opportunities for work emerge or diminish so do the social relations emerge around these opportunities. Whether it is building identity around specific productions or choosing certain careers after school, these contributions paint a broad and complex world of work relating to children and youth.

## Children's Rights

The special protection and care that all children are entitled to as a basic human right is addressed in the scholarly works falling under this theme. The scholars, however, do not all agree on the various rights and entitlements children have, showing that each has to be considered under very specific cultural and geographical contexts. Certain assumptions inherent in the way children's rights have been worded are discussed in view of the socioeconomic and cultural realities of many African communities. Kristen Cheney's research in Uganda helps us understand the process of moving an international discourse on children's rights to a local context where nation-building and development intersect with ideas about childhood and citizenship. Cheney argues that children in Africa evade the conventional definitions of childhood espoused by rights bodies because 'childhood can and should be analyzed as a productive social category integral to — rather than separate from — broader social relations.[19] If, as Cheney shows, child rights in Africa are a result of international discourses on rights and personhood, how do we get to understand the realities of rights of children that can endure beyond specific internationally-sanctioned projects? This complexity may explain the disconnect observed by Adeleke in Nigeria between the offence of rape and the constitutional provisions that define it. As a result social norms that assume a permanently-implied consent by a wife to her husband's sexual advances makes it difficult to reconcile the law and social norms. This seemingly tug-of-war between rights and social norms is also present in areas affecting children such as in corporal punishment which as Archambault shows is seen in two very different ways that antagonizes the school and parents. Research on children's rights in Africa is thus fraught with many challenges emanating from tensions between locally derived social norms and the transnational discourse of rights shaped by experiences mostly in the West.

## Disabilities

Research on disability among children and youth in Africa is still lagging behind other research areas but as the few works highlighted here show, there is a growing (albeit small) body of research that is seeking to expand the understanding of Africa's broad spectrum of disabilities among children and youth. Even as this research is growing we cannot assume that there is an agreed upon definition of what constitutes disability in African societies and in research projects. As it is with many other research categories, disability is very much defined by social circumstances and contexts. When considering such contexts in defining disability then we can argue that individuals may be regarded as having a disability if they experience (or are perceived by others to experience) physiological or behavioral statuses/processes that are socially identified as problems, illnesses, conditions, or disorders. Disability then exists when people with these conditions experience discrimination on the basis of perceived functional limitations in their specific cultural contexts. In many African communities care and resources to assist children with developmental and other forms of disabilities are very limited and in some cases almost absent as shown by Shumba in the case of Botswana where there are very few educational institutions and programs to deal with children with disabilities. Mental health challenges, physical challenges, speech and hearing challenges, all compound the services provided for children especially in educational institutions in Africa. Nyirinkindi argues that educational curriculum in Uganda has developed a language that perpetuates discrimination and victimization of children with disabilities in schools. For these kinds or complications to be heavily present within a phenomenon that has already received very little research attention there is real reason for concern.

## *Early Childhood Care and Development*

This section focuses on scholarly work on the overall well-being of children as it relates to nutrition and the related issues of health. Authors address such diverse issues as how the gender of the household head affects the nutritional quality of the children in the household, school feeding programs and their effect on child school attendance and overall learning, nutrition and disease control, and many others. This section is also related to that on mortality and some of the entries here could fall under that theme and vice versa. I organize this category into three related topics because child mortality and morbidity have a strong bearing and relationship to nurturing practices. With over half of the world's children who die annually before the age of five coming from Africa and there being many incidences of diseases associated with children such as diarrhea and pneumonia, there are scholars trying to provide explanations and descriptions of these occurrences based on region, age, and socioeconomic practices.

The items included in this section address a broad spectrum of issues related to child mortality and some of the sociocultural caregiving and economic factors that may shape the overall health of the children. Authors discuss issues of choices made by breastfeeding mothers based on income, the role played by standards of living on childhood health in general, and the effects of war on child mortality. Ethnographic research elsewhere has show the close relations between on the one hand a mother's overall health and her ability to provide breast milk for her children and on the other the economic incentives for feeding her child on other foods readily available but not necessarily nutritious for a growing child. Sonia Patten's work in Malawi working on a United States Agency for International Aid (USAID) program revealed that many rural Malawi children were not getting enough protein because their mothers were weaning them off after about two years and supplementing mother's milk with porridge.[20] Access to better sources of protein for their children would have improved their children's health in Malawi and Sonia and her team tried to improve children's nutrition by introducing milk goats in the communities but later found that without holistic sources of resources for other household needs, the goats were often sold. Such information on how nurturing affects mortality and morbidity cannot be fully accessed through surveys and questionnaires. Many of the works placed in this section show that high child mortality is linked to economic status of their households as well as the effects of diseases such as HIV/AIDS.

This theme brings together scholarship on education and schooling as a way of highlighting one of the most critical areas of child and youth socialization in contemporary Africa. From questions of why children do not attend school to the role school plays in caring for those with HIV/AIDS and to cultural factors shaping school attendance, the research entries included under this section allow for a rich understanding of education and schooling as a critical part of the sociocultural realities of Africa's children today. Schools are important centers for socializing children in any community but more so in places where the curriculum and school culture tend to be very different from what is available at home or within the indigenous culture. The cultural milieu of the school that shapes the relations participants have with authority, the specific priorities established for each one's success, the degree of formality and the different modes of address, and the set rules that shape conduct within and outside school, all create an institutional culture that quite often clash with home cultures. How does a student in a school interpret the notion of respect when he/she is trained that to show respect to elders or those in authority requires standing up instead of the practice of kneeling or bowing down that is practiced at home? Such a student will have to navigate these two different worlds very carefully. The same can be said of the school curriculum, which quite often is not based on the socioeconomic or cultural experiences of the student's home culture but rather on cultural practices quite alien to the student.

## *Fertility, Sexuality, and Reproductive Health*

Most discussions of fertility, sexuality, and reproductive health in Africa today are tied to the challenges brought by HIV/AIDS. Indeed, the bulk of research that is carried out in these areas is often tied to HIV/AIDS. There are other questions being pursued in this research as shown in the selected works under this theme including why women have a certain number of children, when they should have children, when youth should discuss and engage in sexual intercourse and when and how youth access resources for sexually transmitted infections. These and many other questions allow us to look at some of the areas of research interest in this theme as well as in the area of sexual behavior. The topic of sexuality is not easily presented or debated in public in many African communities but the challenges of HIV/AIDS have forced many communities to start engaging with such issues, albeit reluctantly. As more and more communities transition from tradition modes of family, reproductive health and adolescent sexual behavior have become more prevalent. Adolescent sexual behavior not only has repercussions for emotional and physical health but also shapes behavior and socioeconomic relations in many African societies. Vulnerable children have been forced into sexual activities that they would otherwise not pursue. With this vulnerability comes other social repercussions including teenage pregnancy and sexually transmitted infections. Even in such challenging contexts, researchers have to be willing to push some of the received research norms surrounding sexual behaviour among children and youth. Many scholars working in this area of research have, for instance, focused on what is termed as 'survival sex' whereby vulnerable girls engage in sexual activity in order to get material resources for their own survival. Within a context of limited economic opportunities and the threat of the AIDS pandemic, many girls' engagement in survival sex is all the more troubling. This focus on girls has, however, obscured similar challenges faced by boys. As Chris Lockhart's research shows, even though survival sex as a male phenomenon may not be related to the direct acquisition of some material resource, 'it may be indirectly related through participation in sexual activity as the result of peer pressure or the need to fit in, which in turn may have direct implications for acquiring material resources'.[21] Challenging certain taken for granted research approaches to sexuality and reproductive health can yield more nuanced studies of children and youth in Africa.

## HIV/AIDS and Orphans

HIV and AIDS have been the most researched and written about topics in the last ten years of research on children and youth in Africa. When this is combined with the effects the disease has on the lives of children, affecting them physiologically as carriers of the virus as well as socially as orphan left behind after death of their caregivers following the disease, one can predict continued focus on the topic for the next decade as well. This time around, however, there will most likely be more focus on child survival given the growing availability of medical resources to keep those with HIV/AIDS active and healthy. Many families and communities are heavily burdened by HIV/AIDS and poverty but children in most African communities are 'connected through broad, extended family networks with a variety of kinship arrangements — matrilineality, patrilineality and marriages across both lines — which ensure that most children who lose or have ailing parents do not fend for themselves'.[22] Despite this social reality, the reported growth of orphans in Africa has reached an unprecedented rate probably because of the now accepted definition of an orphan as 'a child who has lost one or both parents through death'.[23] This definition has defined the kinds of programs, policies and even research carried out in much of Africa. In Malawi where Freidus carried out here research matrilineal descent systems often have children living with their mothers and traditionally 'divorce rates are high, remarriage is common, and men tend to be mobile'.[24] Indeed even in South Africa, research shows that children labeled 'orphans' many times still live with their mothers, with lives not dramatically different from when they were living with both parents.[25] Research in Africa on orphans has to, therefore, be grounded in the social realities of the communities being studied rather than assume a universal definition of orphanhood that is mobilized through powerful organizations such as UNICEF. One has to ask whether focusing on the concept of orphanhood is motivated by external research and funding agendas or by local realities because in the matrilineal communities Freidus worked 'whether fathers have died or moved away is often irrelevant to many children, who remain in the care of their mothers'.[26]

## Media, Popular Culture and Representation

The way children and youth have been conceptualized and represented in Africa has quite often been mediated through literature, music, theater, film, and even proverbs. Representations of children and youth that connote such terms or phrases as 'risky', 'rebellious', 'lost', 'vulnerable', or 'innovative', among others emanate not from what youth themselves say about themselves but what others say about them. Granted that some youth do live up to these characterizations (but so are many other people including adults) that does not mean that such generalizations are valid. The question is then how novels, films, and other forms of folklore have represented African youth and children in the last ten years. How has radio shaped youth social practices and how do children use media to construct certain images of self and others? These questions form the main thrust of the published works represented in this section. With increased global exchange and flows of goods, services, and products and the readiness of many African youth to embrace new forms of representation and new media, scholars are finding that traditional modes of representing youth and children in Africa are constantly changing. Through this media as well as other opportunities allow youth and children to self-represent. The influx of film, music, dress, and even magazines from outside one's local space have led to new ways of seeing the world and self for many youth in Africa. Some of the scholarly works under this theme have described, discussed and analyzed various ways through which (mostly) youth in Africa use popular culture to create their own identities based on lived as well as imagined experiences. Others also critique those experiences.

16

## *Parenting and Children's Relations with Fathers*

It has now become clearer that the care and teaching of young children, which has traditionally been seen as 'women's work', is no longer valid. The number of fathers solely responsible for the care of their children is growing but researchers are also challenging certain assumptions about fathers' relationships with their children. As Robert Morrell has argued, 'the position of fatherhood cannot be measured simplistically in terms of his physical absence or presence. A father might well be physically present, but emotionally absent, or physically absent but emotionally supportive'.[27] More research findings from South Africa also show that children's co-residence with their fathers is neither an accurate nor a sufficient indicator that they are receiving paternal financial support because children are as likely to receive financial support from fathers who are not even members of the same household as from fathers with whom they are co-resident and that once children receive support from their fathers for any part of their lives they are likely to receive support consistently throughout their lives.[28] These are the realities of social relationships that scholars ought to continually pay attention to especially in circumstances where the relationships children and youth have with their parents are involved. What dynamics are there in households where both parents are working and have to relegate most of their childcare to other individuals? What about in households where mothers are the sole breadwinners? What influence do fathers/men have on children's lives in different parts of Africa, and what is the impact of the absence of fathers (due to divorce, migrant work schedules or death) in the lives of children and the social dynamics and meanings surrounding men's increased roles in the socialization of children? In this growing field of research the scholarly works selected under this theme try to contend with answers to these questions while also focusing on the more common mode of parenting associated with mothers. The topic of fatherhood and their role in the socialization of children is gaining important ground in Africa and is one area that needs even more attention in the future given the different realities already displayed in the works explored in this monograph.

## Research On/With Children and Youth

What are the trends in research on children and youth in Africa today? What are the ethical considerations and/or challenges of conducting research with children? Do children have the necessary emotional and social abilities to make decisions about being part of a research project? How do agendas and research questions derived from adults' own experience enter into questions asked of children during research? What advantages are there for using children and youth as researchers themselves not just the subjects of research? These are complex questions that require a thorough understanding not only of the context of research but also of one's own subject position as a researcher. One such area of self awareness involves a researcher's understanding of the ethics of research and the need for gaining consent from children or youth one is working with during research. Jo Boyden has provided a very important critique of the practice of seeking and receiving informed consent during research with children especially those in conflict situations. Boyden argues that 'while the need for informed consent may seem self-evident, it is, in practice, very difficult to achieve in the case of children . . . partly because the researcher, as an adult, negotiates with the research subjects from a position of superiority'.[29] This power position often plays into the prevalent practice in many African societies of socializing children to mostly be 'seen not heard' and where adult decisions inform children's activities whether children agree with them or not. Any adult researcher working with children has to be attentive to these ethical issues and shape the research to be minimize this sociocultural bias in collecting data among children. Some of the authors whose work is highlighted in this section do explore these tensions and even go ahead to show the value of reflexively reworking some of the ethical practices of fieldwork highlighted by researchers from the north. The work of Tatek Abebe (in this monograph) is a case in point here.

## Rituals, Beliefs, and Spirituality

The way a community or society regards and interacts with its members is shaped by certain values and beliefs about the world and human's relations and place in it. Perceptions about children, their health, their personalities, as well as their future, are often shaped by culturally-determined values and beliefs. In many African cultural traditions, the world is not divided up into separate spheres of the sacred and secular common in many Western societies. The spiritual world is very much part of the secular world and one does not see much separation between the two. Many causes of experiences of the everyday have been often been attributed to spiritual forces in many African societies. Death, diseases, accidents, and success can all be attributed to some extent to some spiritual force beyond one's human manipulation and their solutions tend to be referred to the spiritual realm. Many have been cases, especially in Southern Africa, of men having sex with virgins (for what has been termed 'virgin cure') as a way of curing HIV/AIDS. Many are also cases of accusations of witchcraft and power of the occult assigned to children. These ideas and practices are very much tied to worldviews that use traditional African belief systems to respond to many of contemporary challenges facing societies and communities in the continent. Scholarly work included under this theme has addressed some of these issues, showing how children seen as inhabited by spirits are seen in negative light in their societies, how the birth of twins often pose challenges to some communities and the need for specific rituals to prepare twins for acceptance into their communities, and other rituals carried out for children after birth in order to protect them from disease. Clearly the traditional African worldview continues to engage with a scientific world in various ways and scholars interested in this area of research will have to continue digging deeper not only into the belief systems of members of various communities but also the ways such beliefs interact with new ideas and practices brought by modernity.

## *Street Children, Ex-combatants, and Rehabilitation*

Children living without any real adult supervision is in itself a challenge but more challenging is the phenomenon of children living on their own on the streets of urban centers where life is less guided by kinship ties and more by transactional realities. Children who also served in combat contexts and are now seeking new ways of reentering mainstream society find themselves in similar situations as do street children. In the works listed under this theme, scholars are looking critically at how children who have on one hand been seen as vulnerable can be on the other quite independent and disruptive of the expected life trajectories they should take within their communities. Urban life in Africa in general continues to provide many complicated avenues for these kinds of studies. Scholars whose works have been included in this section also grapple with various forms of urban life especially as they relate to youth and children. They discuss and analyze factors leading to children going on the streets, the mechanics of negotiating social relations on the streets, the realities of living in rehabilitation contexts after years of being in armed combat, and the insights we can get about urban life by observing these inhabitants. As scholars discuss whether children join guerrilla armies willingly or not we are starting to see issues about children and youth agency emerging and complicating the once assumed vulnerability of children discourses as well. We see more and more scholars interrogating the constructions of children as vulnerable and in need of adult care and protection, and as a result revealing a more complex understanding of the role children and youth play in public life. This understanding has to, however, be anchored in contextualized qualitative studies. As David Rosen has noted when writing about child soldiers, 'the 'problem' of child soldiers, widely regarded as a modern international humanitarian and human rights crisis, derives not from any new phenomenon of young people being present on the battlefield but rather, from an emerging transnational 'politics of age' that shapes the concept of 'childhood' in international law'.[30]

Central to this discourse of child soldiers as well as child labor and child-headed households is part of what these politics of age, which according to Rosen denotes 'the use of age categories by different international, regional and local actors to advance particular political and ideological positions'.[31] The larger international framing of what constitutes childhood, which in turn shapes how African children are written about does not engage the diverse contexts and practices that these children go through. Indeed, calculated funding priorities and research agendas, childhood and its specific identity has assumed a globalized rather than localized definition. Every African society has its own understanding of childhood (and some may be shared by many societies) but such an understanding and its consequent definitions have been nullified by these global definitions that assume universal experiences and understandings of childhood. In the scholarly works represented in this monograph we see numerous examples of these universalized notions of childhood and youth but in there are some examples that deviate from this model and offer some localized study that allows us to see how life is experienced, expressed, and mobilized by children and youth in ways that cannot fit into any neat analytical categories. It is my hope that in the next decade of research on children and youth in Africa, there will be more scholarship on these diverse perspectives of children and youth and fewer ones following the universalizing model.

## Search Strategy

Searches for the bibliography included here were compiled from online sources some of which have been listed at the end of the bibliographic entries in this monograph. All of the indices provided many publications mostly written in English, some in French, and very few in Afrikaans. The keywords 'child' 'children' 'childhood' and 'youth' were combined with 'Africa' in the searches and limited to the specific timeline of between 2001 and 2011. Given these search criteria and strategies, and in spite of the extensive effort to include all relevant studies produced in the set time frame, it is likely that some relevant research studies were excluded from this review because they were inaccessible to the author at the time of compiling the bibliography. As a result, some important work may have been overlooked.

## Structure of Monograph

Studies are categorized in twelve (12) different themes as follows: Agency and Generational Relations; Child Labour and Child-Headed Households; Children's Rights; Disabilities; Early Childhood Care and Development; Fertility and Reproductive Health; HIV/AIDS and Orphans; Media and Representation; Parenting and Children's Relations with Fathers; Research On/With Children and Youth; Rituals, Beliefs, and Spirituality; and Street Children, Ex-Combatants, and Rehabilitation. These themes were chosen to assist in grouping together works that are related in their overall focus. All entries are listed by name of first author and ordered alphabetically. A few aspects of each study were selected for inclusion in the summary, including the main focus of the study and some of the key findings.

## Notes

1. Henderson, Patti (2002) *Annotated Bibliography on Childhood, With Emphasis on Africa: Outline, General Findings, and Research Recommendations*. Dakar, Senegal: CODESRIA, pp.1

2. See, for instance, Victor Muzvidziwa's paper under 'child labour and child-headed households' in this monograph in which he argues that many children have to work for survival and the issue is not whether they should work but rather under what conditions they work.

3. American sociologist Viviana Zelizer traces this economically 'useless' and emotionally 'priceless', modern American child in her book titled *Pricing the Priceless Child: The Changing Social Value of Children*, New York: Basic Books, 1985.

4. Jo Boyden and J. Berry, eds., 2004, *Children and Youth on the Frontline: Ethnography, Armed Conflict and Displacement*. Oxford: Berghahn Books, pp. xvii.

5. See a sampling of Dr. Bame Nsamenang's scholarly works at this website http://www.unige.ch/fapse/SSE/teachers/dasen/ Nsamenang.htm and also visit the website for the Human Development Resource Center that he co-founded and directs here http://thehdrc.org/index.html. I am grateful to Dr. Auma Okwany for introducing me to Dr. Nsemenang's work.

6. Nsamenang, B., 2006, 'Human Ontogenesis: An Indigenous African View on Development and Intelligence', *International Journal of Psychology*, Vol. 41 (4): 293-297, pp. 294.

7. Ibid., p. 295.

8. Case study shared in Alan Pence and Kofi Marfo, 2008, 'Early Childhood Development in Africa: Interrogating Constraints of Prevailing Knowledge Bases', *International Journal of Psychology*, Vol 43 (2):78-87, p. 85.

9. Ibid.

10. See, Jennifer Keys Adair, 'Ethnographic knowledge for early childhood', available at http://www.aaanet.org/sections/cae/ pdf%20files/Ethnography_&_ECE_Brief_Final_Adair2.pdf accessed January 19, 2012.

11. See Nsamenang, B. and Therese Tchombe, eds., 2011, *Handbook of African Educational Theories and Practices: A Generative Teacher Educstion Curriculum*, Human Development Research Center, available at http://thehdrc.org/Handbook%20of%20African%20Educational%20Theories%20and%20Practices.pdf.

Okwany, A., Elizabeth Ngutuku, and Arthur Muchangi, eds., 2011, *The Role of Local Knowledge and Culture in Child Care in Africa: A Sociological Study of Several Ethnic Groups in Kenya and Uganda*, Edwin Mellen Press.

12. See, Robert Levine, 2004, 'Challenging Expert Knowledge: Findings from an African Study of Infant Care and Development', in *Childhood and Adolescence: Cross-Cultural Perspectives and Applications*, edited by Uwe P. Gielen and Jaipul Roopnarine, pp 149-165. Westport, CT: Praeger.

13. See, Johnson-Hanks, Jennifer, 2002. 'On the Limits of Life Stages in Ethnography: Toward a Theory of Vital Conjunctions', *American Anthropologist*, Vol. 104 (3): 865-880.

14. See, Kristen Cheney, 2007, *Pillars of the Nation: Child Citizens and Ugandan National Development*. Chicago: University of Chicago Press, pp. 55.

15. Boyden and Berry (2004:xiii).

16. Ibid. 2004:xiv.

17. See, Ntarangwi, M., Mills, D., and Babiker, M., eds., 2006, 'Introduction', to *African Anthropologies: History, Practice and Critique*. London: Zed Books and Dakar, Senegal: CODESRIA.

18. Muzvidziwa, Victor, 2006, 'Child Labour or Child Work?: Whither Policy', *Institute of African Studies Research Review*, Vol. 22 (1):23-33.

19. See, Kristen Cheney (2007:16).

20. See, Sonia Patten, 2004, 'Medical Anthropology: Improving Nutrition in Malawi', in *Conformity and Conflict: Readings in Cultural Anthropology*, 11th edition, eds. Spradley and McCurdy. Allyn and Bacon, pp. 405-414.

21. Chris Lockhart, 2002, 'Kunyenga, 'Real Sex' and Survival: Assessing the Risk of HIV Infection Among Urban Street Boys in Tanzania', *Medical Anthropology Quarterly*, Vol. 16 (3): 294-411, p. 2.

22. Freidus, Andrea, 2010, 'Raising Malawi's Children: Unanticipated Outcomes Associated with Institutionalised Care', *Children & Society*, Vol. 24:293-303, p. 294.

23. UNICEF, 2009, Orphans. http://www.unicef.org/media/media_ 45290.html, accessed February 25, 2012.

24. Freidus, andrea, 2010, "Saving' Malawi: Faithful Responses to Orphans and Vulnerable Children', *Napa Bulletin*, Vol. 33: 50-67, p. 54.

25. See, for instance, Meintjes, H., and S. Giese, 2006, 'Spinning the Epidemic: The Making of Mythologies of Orphanhood in the Context of AIDS', Childhood 13(3):407–430.

26. Ibid.

27. Morrell, Robert, 2007, 'Fathers, Fatherhood and Masculinity in South Africa', In *Baba: Men and Fatherhood in South Africa*, edited by Linda Richter and Robert Morrell, South Africa: HSRC Press, pp. 13-24, p. 18.

28. Madhavan, S., N. Townsend, and A. Garey, "Absent Breadwiners': Father-Child Connections and Paternal Support in Rural South Africa', *Journal of Southern African Studies*, Vol. 34 (3):647-663.

29. Jo Boyden, 2000, 'Conducting Research with War-Affected and Displaced Children: Ethics & Methods', *Cultural Survival Quarterly* Vol. 24, no. 2 available at http://www.culturalsurvival.org/ publications/cultural-survival-quarterly/united-states/conducting-research-war-affected-and-displace accessed January 23, 2012.

30. David Rosen (2007) 'Child Soldiers, International Humanitarian Law and the Globalization of Childhood', *American Anthropologist*, Vol. 109 (2): 296-306, p. 296.

31. Ibid.

# Part I

**Child/Youth Agency and Perceptions/
Reflections**

## 1.   Babo, Alfred

2009, 'Faillite de l'État et Administration de L'espace Public Politique par es 'Jeunes Patriotes' en Côte d'Ivoire', *Africa Development*, Vol. 34, no. 3/4, pp. 27-45.

Focuses on youth in Ivory Coast becoming politically engaged because of failed state apparatus to provide social, economic, and political leadership. Author focuses on the 'Agora' youth movement, which emerged at the break of war in 2002. Youth try to engage with public space by restructuring it through spontaneous or organized protests that provide them opportunities to enter in public discourse about politics and governance.

## 2.   Badjoo, Lucien and Katia Clarens

2005, J'étais Enfant-Soldat: Le Récit Poignant d'une Enfance Africaine. Paris: Plon.

This book co-authored by a journalist (Clarens) and an ex-combatant (Badjoko) provides an account of a young Zairian ex-combatant who was committed to twelve years in Kabila's troops during the civil war against the Mobutu regime. This book provides information about internal power struggles in the movement and even the role played by Rwanda in the changes in the leadership of AFDL and LDK movements fighting for control of DR Congo.

## 3.   Bahi, Aghi

2003, 'La 'Sorbonne' d'Abidjan: Rêve de Démocratie ou Naissance d'un Espace Public', *Revue Africaine de Sociologie / African Sociological Review*, Vol. 7, No. 1, pp. 47-63.

The author discusses the recent development of social forums in Abidjan spearheaded by youth in which they talk about politics. The first of these is named Sorbonne Plateau, after the famous Parisian university. The author interrogates the meaning of this phenomenon and hypothesizes that this may mean a new way of using public space in the new context of a multiparty system. Based on the author's observations and interviews with youth in Abidjan, the article describes the typical political forum and shows that the meaning constructed by the actors of democracy is an 'authentic' one in which individuals freely discuss city affairs and express their opinions. The return to multiparty politics, but especially the new constitution after the military-civilian transition in 2000 has helped spread this idea of free speech in young men from both rural and urban locales and is shaping their engagement with public space.

## 4.    Behrend, Heike

2002, 'I am Like a Movie Star in My Street': Photographic Self-Creation in Postcolonial Kenya', in *Postcolonial subjectivities in Africa*, ed. by Richard Werbner, London: Zed Books: pp. 44-62.

This chapter deals with popular photography and postcolonial subjectivities in Kenya. For Kenyan urban youth, there is a radically 'desired other', the African American from the ghetto with his fashion, body poses, slang, and hip hop music. The author shows, on the basis of the example of 18-year old Peter Mwasunguchi from Mombasa, how the medium of photography is used as a technique for self-creation by urban Kenyan youth. She examines the ways in which Peter and his friends enter into social exchange around images of themselves as 'the desired other'. Stylized after the African American, their images obliterate the friends' own ethnic differences and thus represent them renewed as autonomous individuals.

## 5.    Benga, Ndiouga A.

2001, 'Entre Jérusalem et Babylone: Jeunes et Espace Public à Dakar', *Autrepart*, No. 18, pp. 169-178.

The author discusses the challenges and creativity of inhabiting urban space for youth in Dakar in what he calls a new urban order — where violence is used to affirm one's space as well as nationalist discourses shaped by local and international aspirations. He finds that artists use paintings and music to reclaim this social space as these youth try to avoid being sidelined as well as trying to make sense of their own tangled lives.

## 6.    Biggeri, Mario and Anich, Rudolf

2009, 'The Deprivation of Street Children in Kampala: Can the Capability Approach and Participatory Methods Unlock a New Perspective in Research and Decision Making?' *Monde en Développement, 2009,* Vol. 37, No. 146, pp. 73-93.

The authors start on the premise that children are no longer seen merely as recipients of services or beneficiaries of protective measures, but rather as subjects of rights and participants in actions affecting them. This implies a change in the approach also towards vulnerable children in research and decision making. The paper explores the deprivation of street children in Kampala (Uganda), through the innovative combination of the Amatya Sen's capability approach and participatory methods, moving away from the lens of children as needy but rather as resourceful agents involved in solving their own problems.

## 7.    Cheney, Kristen E.

2004, 'Village Life is Better than Town Life': Identity, Migration, and development in the lives of Ugandan child citizens', *African Studies Review,* Vol. 47, no. 3, pp. 1-22.

Looks at children's understanding of rural-urban life based on experiences, imagination, and knowledge. The author argues that the influenced of urban-rural migration has changed urban schoolchildren's notions of family and kinship, and the national government's 'development-through-education' campaign, leading them to imagine 'the village' both as an integral imaginary space of ethnic identity origination and a location for fulfillment of national citizenship through development.

## 8.    Cheney, Kristen E.

2007, *Pillars of the Nation: Child Citizens and Ugandan National Development,* Chicago: The University of Chicago Press.

This book explores the daily contradictions children face as they try to find their places amid the country's rapidly changing social conditions. The author draws on detailed life histories of several children to that children and childhood are being redefined by the desires of a young country struggling to position itself in the international community. Through an analysis of children's rights ideology, national government strategy, and children's everyday concerns, the author also shows how these young citizens are vitally linked to the global political economy as they navigate the pitfalls and possibilities for a brighter tomorrow.

## 9.    Diouf, Mamadou

2003, 'Engaging Postcolonial Cultures: African Youth and Public Space', *African Studies Review*, Vol. 46, no. 2, pp. 1-12.

Young people are emerging as one of the central concerns of African studies today. Located at the heart of both analytical apparatuses and political action, they have also become a preoccupation of politicians, social workers and communities in Africa. Several factors seem to have been involved in this increased focus on youth. This paper makes two major observations: First, the youthful population of Africa has been growing and their integration into society has had enormous economic, cultural, political and social consequences, and second, the condition of young people in Africa is heavily influenced by the interaction between local and global pressures. This has led the construction of African youth as a threat as their bodies, behaviour, sexuality, and their pleasure, are no longer easily contained within existing state and political apparatuses. The author concludes that this new situation has consequences for several issues, the most important of which are the redefinition of the relationships between identity and citizenship, the metamorphoses of the processes of socialization, the production of new forms of inequality, and the extraordinary mutation of the chronological and psychological constructions of the passage from youth to adulthood.

## 10.    Durham, Deborah

2004, 'Disappearing Youth: Youth as a Social Shifter in Botswana', *American Ethnologist*, Vol 31, Issue 4, pp. 589 – 605.

This article explores the discourses of youth in Botswana, focusing the analysis on 1995 protests over the murder of a student. The author argues that youth should be examined as a social shifter: When invoked, youth indexes sets of social relationships that are dynamic and constructed in the invocation. As people argue over who youth are and how they behave, they index shifting relationships of power and authority, responsibility and capability, agency and autonomy, and the moral configurations of society.

## 11.  Ebrahim, H. and D. Francis

2008, 'You Said, 'Black Girl': Doing Difference in Early Childhod', *Africa Education Review*, Vol. 5, no. 2, pp. 274-287.

This paper based on research in Kwazulu-Natal, focuses on children's constructions of childhood especially around issues of race and gender. Using data produced through observations, storytelling, and persona dolls, the author argue that, although young children reproduce multiple social realities they encounter in their daily lives, they are active subjects in constructing differences. This practice of story telling with persona dolls also provides opportunities for young children to talk about their experiences with regards to social, racial, and ethnic differences.

## 12.  Etherton, Michael, ed.

2006, *African Theater: Youth*, Oxford: James Currey.

An edited volume that brings together essays focusing on the voices of the young people on ho they are using theatre and performance to struggle for their rights and for changes in their lives. The volume presents studies of theatre that young Africans have made and performed to audiences across the continent, providing a wide range of work, much of which depicts the crises that young Africans face as they enter the world of adult relationships and compromises.

## 13.  Evans, Ruth

2010, 'We are Managing Our Own Lives . . . ': Life Transitions and Care in Sibling-Headed Households Affected by AIDS in Tanzania and Uganda', Online publication, http://onlinelibrary.wiley.com/doi/10.1111/j.1475-4762.2010.00954.x/full

Explores the ways that young people express their agency and negotiate complex life course transitions according to gender, age and inter- and intra-generational norms in sibling-headed households affected by AIDS in East Africa.

## 14. Evers, Sandra J.T.M., Catrien Notermans, and Erik van Ommering, (eds)

2011, *Not Just Victim: the Child as Catalyst and Witness of Contemporary Africa*, Leiden and Boston: Brill Publishers.

The authors in this volume argue that children are dynamic contributors to the shaping of contemporary Africa. Through novel and unorthodox ethnographic research methods, each chapter provides insights into children's perspectives on kinship, work, caring, health, migration and conflict, shedding light on children's views and the vital roles they play in the emerging Africa of tomorrow. The volume avoids portraying African children as passive actors, mere extensions of adult societies, and receptors of culture, but rather as active agents in their own lives.

## 15. Hamer, Magali Chelpi-Den

2009, 'Le mythe du jeune désœuvré : analyse des interventions DDR en Côte d'Ivoire', *Afrique contemporaine*, No. 232, pp. 39-55.

This article explores how young civilians who have been militarized by the Ivorian conflict have made use of a standard instrument of rehabilitation interventions commonly used in international post-conflict, and examines the reintegration options offered under a pilot project to reintegrate ex -combatants. The author uses the perspective of these young people, to answer a number of questions including: what are the advantages and disadvantages of participating in such a project? What are the economic and social issues that have motivated such participation? How do the youth use the prospects of rehabilitation that the project offers them and how do they integrate (or not) with other more lucrative options outside the project? To what extent does participation in the project facilitate their social and economic reintegration? Most of the data is based on 200 semi-structured interviews in Guiglo and Man, the main strongholds of pro-government militias and rebels in western Ivory Coast.

## 16. Honwana, Alcinda and Filip de Boeck, (eds)

2005, *Makers & Breakers: Children & Youth in Postcolonial Africa*, Oxford: James Currey; Dakar: CODESRIA; Trenton: Africa World Press.

The chapters in this volume on youth in Africa are revised versions of papers presented at two conferences held in 1999 in Cape Town, South Africa, in June and in Leuven, Belgium, in November. Some additional chapters were solicited by the editors. The volume addresses the dynamics of both local and transnational forces that are affecting African young people today. Youth are portrayed as both perpetrators and victims in civil conflict, as leaders and led in movements of political and religious renewal, and as innovators and dupes in the globalization of culture.

## 17.   Jones, Jeremy

2009, 'It's not Normal But It's Common': Elopement, Marriage and the Mediated Recognition of Youth Identity in Harare, Zimbabwe, *CODESRIA Bulletin*, Nos 3 & 4, pp. 3-14.

This paper argues that marriage and the creation of independent households are not only the lynchpin for youth futures, but for societal stability more generally and yet it is the inability of youth to fulfill these normative transitions that makes them liminal and dangerous. Using data collected in Zimbabwe the author shows that these normative demands of social adulthood are clearly important to the lives of youth, but they must be properly situated in a wider picture of how practical relations are formed on the ground especially given the socioeconomic constraints these youth face.

## 18.   Kagwanja, Peter Mwangi

2006, "Power to 'Uhuru'": Youth identity and Generational Politics in Kenya's 2002 Elections', *African Affairs*, Vol. 104, no. 418, pp. 51-75.

This article examines how when faced with the challenge of a new, multi-ethnic political coalition, Kenya's President Daniel arap Moi shifted the axis of the 2002 electoral contest from ethnicity to the politics of generational conflict. This strategy, the author argues, backfired, ripping his party wide open and resulting in its humiliating defeat in the December 2002 general elections. Nevertheless, the discourse of a generational change of guard as a blueprint for a more accountable system of governance won the support of some youth movements like the predominantly Kikuyu Mungiki movement while the opposition movement's leadership exploited the generational discourse in an effort to capture power. Examining these dual manipulations of generational and ethnic identities in patrimonial politics, the article argues that the instrumentalization of ethnicity in African politics has its corollary in the concomitant instrumentalization of other identities - race, class, gender, clan, age and religion.

### 19.  Kamper, Gerrit and Miemsie Steyn

2007, 'My Toekoms in Suid-Afrika: Perspektiewe en Verwagtings van die Afrikaanssprekende Jeug', *Tydskrif vir Geesteswetenskappe*, Jg., 47, nr. 4, pp. 516-530

Examines perspectives and expectations of Afrikaans-Speaking South African youth on their future orientation seeking to answer the question: To what extent is the brown youth skeptical about their future in South Africa? The research applied questionnaire to 432 11th grade students and found that respondents were generally positive about the realization of their ideal future in South Africa.

### 20.  Kapteijns, Lidwien and Maryan Muuse Boqor

2009, 'Memories of a Mogadishu Childhood, 1940-1964: Maryan Muuse Boqor and the Women Who Inspired Her', *The International Journal of African Historical Studies*, Vol. 42, no. 1, pp. 105-116.

Paper about an adult woman (Maryan Muuse Boqor) who reflects on her childhood in Somalia through interviews recorded in 2001 in Boston, where she was resettled as a refugee. This paper presents the memories of her childhood in Mogadishu during the period 1940-1964, providing a set of reminiscences and reflections on the values Maryan's family members, as well as many of their Somali contemporaries, held and passed on to their children. These values then find challenges when applied to a new context of living in the USA.

### 21.  Löfgren, Johanna, Josephat Byamugisha, Per Tillgren, and Birgitta Rubenson

2009, 'The Perspectives of in-School Youths in Kampala, Uganda, on the Role of Parents in HIV Prevention', *African Journal of AIDS Research*, Vol. 8, no. 2, pp. 193-200.

This is a qualitative study that explores how young Ugandans perceive and experience the role of parents in preventing the spread of HIV among youth. Data were gathered from semi-structured face-to-face interviews with 16 in-school youths, ages 18-20, residing in Kampala. A key finding is that the youths perceived parenting styles as influencing HIV prevention among youths and identified several harmful consequences from a lack of parental guidance or inadequate parenting and they discussed the gains of parental support in terms of assisting HIV prevention among youths.

## 22.  Mukamugambira, Pascasie & Kwaku Osei-Hwedie

2007, 'Factors Influencing Attitudes of Botswana Youth Towards Manual Work: Implications for Employment', *Journal of Social Development in Africa*, Vol. 22, no. 2, pp. 107-135.

This paper examines attitudes of youth towards manual work, factors that contributed to these attitudes, and the implications of these attitudes for youth employment. It is based on a study of 119 youths, aged 15 to 29 years, working in the construction, domestic and farming sectors in Gaborone (Botswana) and three neighbouring villages. The paper concludes that, generally, youth in Botswana demonstrate positive attitudes towards manual work.

## 23.  Ottenberg, Simon and David A. Binkley, (eds)

2006, *Playful Performers: African Children's Masquerades*, New Brunswick: Transaction Publishers.

Study of children masquerade and the creativity that goes into preparing these activities among children. Contributors to this edited volume describe specific cases of young children's masking in the areas of west, central, and southern Africa, which also happen to be the major areas of adult masquerading. The volume reveals the considerable creativity and ingenuity that children exhibit in preparing costumes, masks and musical instruments, and in playing music, dancing, singing, and acting. The book includes over 50 pages of black and white photographs, which illustrate and elaborate upon the authors' main points and offers a challenging perspective on young children, seeing them as active agents in their own culture rather than passive recipients of culture as taught by parents and other elders.

## 24.  Oumar, Silue

2009, Youth's game-playing in Ivorian Public Space: Involving the Youth of Street Dialogue Spaces in Politics, *CODESRIA Bulletin,* Nos. 3 & 4, pp. 43-50.

This paper discusses street dialogue spaces where young individuals meet to critically look at the latest developments in political events in Ivory Coast. These debates most often take place, as the author describes them, next to public places and involves actors whose actions have an impact on the Ivorian socio-political life. In most cases, the debates are led by jobless and unmarried young men living in the popular suburbs of Abidjan (Yopougon, Abobo, Koumassi). The author concludes that these gatherings, termed 'Agoras and parliaments' take the form of political meetings led by orators who attract audiences in the hundreds and even thousands.

## 25.  Renee, Elisha P.

2005, 'Childhood Memories and Contemporary Parenting in Ekiti, Nigeria', *Africa: Journal of the International African Institute,* Vol. 75, no. 1, pp. 63-82.

Author discusses the practices of using children as a 'deposit' to repay debts owed by families in a process where the lender kept the child until the family repaid all its debt. An older man reflects on this practice, which was outlawed by the British colonial administration because it was regarded child slavery. The author provides an analysis of how such a practice can be likened to modern day child fostering practices and how these activities collectively affect contemporary child bearing and rearing practices.

## 26.  Smuts, Claris, (ed.)

2002, *Letters to Madiba: Voices of South African Children.* Cape Town: Maskew Miller Longman.

This a collection of a selection of letters (out of a total of 800,000) written by South African children regarding what they think about their country, their hopes and dreams, and what they wanted to say to Nelson Mandela, the first president of a democratic South Africa. The selected letters provide a hopeful, inspiring story of pride, optimism and honesty from primary school children, and encapsulates the children's innermost feelings about what it means to grow up in South Africa. The editor includes ideas and activities for teachers and parents at the end of the book.

## 27.   Stears, Michèle

2008, 'Children's Stories: What Knowledge Constitutes Indigenous Knowledge?', *Indilinga*. Vol. 7, no. 2, pp. 132-140.

Provides an analysis of the kind of knowledge produced by children through stories and how that knowledge can be included in the school curriculum. Author finds that much of the content produced by the children is not indigenous and argues that poor socioeconomic conditions may often erode students' ability to value and use indigenous knowledge as a basis for school learning.

## 28.   Trudell, Barbara, Kenneth King, Simon McGrath, and Paul Nugent, (eds)

2002, *Africa's Young Majority*. Edinburgh: Centre of African Studies, University of Edinburgh.

The papers in this volume derive from the conference 'Africa's young majority', which was organized in 2001 by the Centre of African Studies, University of Edinburgh. Containing fourteen papers produced by academics and NGO practitioners working with young people, the volume aspires to present young people not as objects of policy or of research, but rather seeks to capture the vibrancy of young people as actors and agents in so many spheres of social, cultural and political life. Topics covered include sports, popular culture, fighting against apartheid, and dilemmas facing youth in the context of HIV/AIDS.

## 29.   Uchendu, Egodi

2007, 'Recollections of Childhood Experiences During the Nigerian Civil War', *Africa: Journal of the International African Institute*. Vol. 77, no. 3, pp. 393-418.

The paper provides an analysis on the recollections of present-day adults who experienced the crisis of the Nigerian civil war of 1967-70 in their childhood. Data for the paper were gathered by means of a qualitative research methodology, telling the story of the Nigerian civil war as the narrators perceived it in their childhoods. The author provides a discussion that probes the respondents' feelings and responses to the conflict, their lives under hostilities and some of the effects of the war on child survivors. The author then attempts to make sense of continued conflicts in Nigeria through the filter of these recollections.

## 30. UNICEF (United Nations Children's Fund)

2006, 'What Children and Youth Think' Project.

Chronicles the thoughts and concerns of over 4000 children and youth in Southern and Eastern Africa in 2006 regarding their well-being, emotions and environment; their relationships with family and friends; their relationship with their communities, their countries and their leaders; and their perceptions of the issues concerning them. These reports are divided into eight countries and are available online:

## 31. Angola (www.uneca.org/adfv/polls/Angola.pdf)

Botswana (www.uneca.org/adfv/polls/botswana.pdf);

Burundi (www.uneca.org/adfv/polls/Brundi.pdf);

Ethiopia (www.uneca.org/adfv/polls/Ethiopia.pdf);

Malawi (www.uneca.org/adfv/polls/malawi.pdf);

Rwanda (www.uneca.org/adfv/polls/Rwanda.pdf);

Somalia (www.uneca.org/adfv/polls/somalia.pdf); and

Tanzania (www.uneca.org/adfv/polls/Tanzania%20.pdf).

## 32. Uvin, Peter

2007, 'Human Security in Burundi: The View from Below (by youth)'. *African Security Review*, Vol. 16, no. 2, pp. 38-52.

This paper presents the result of hundreds of conversations with ordinary Burundians -foremost but not exclusively youth - about what 'peace' means to them. The aim was to generally learn how, after 13 years of war, (young, male) ordinary Burundians see the future. The interviews were conducted in six different places (rural and urban), representing different situation of life during the war in Burundi. The paper develops a typology of answers people presented - negative peace, positive peace, social peace, peace related to mobility, peace as good governance, peace of mind - and links these popular insights to the human security agenda.

# Part II

## Child Labour and Child-Headed Households

## 33. Abukari, Ziblim

2007, 'Dimensions of Youth Unemployment in Ghana: a Public Policy Perspective', *Journal of Social Development in Africa*, Vol. 22, no. 2, pp. 83-105.

This paper provides a general overview of youth unemployment in Ghana dues to such factors as underdevelopment of the economies, low literacy rates, a small and underresourced private sector, rural-urban migration and low-quality education that equips young people with poor skills. The author then calls for strong political will and commitment on the part of the Ghanaian government, to address the challenges associated with youth unemployment in the country.

## 34. Adejuwon, Grace A.

2008, 'Market Women's Attitude Towards Child Labour in Nigeria: the Influence of Parental and Environmental Factors'. *Journal of Social Development in Africa*, Vol. 23, no. 2, pp. 157-184.

This paper examines the influence of parental and social environment factors on the attitude of market women towards child labour. The study population consisted of 300 market women from two major markets in Ibadan, Oyo State, Nigeria. The research instrument used was a questionnaire. The results show that market women in polygamous settings, those with no education, those living in rural and semi-rural areas, as well as those with a low level of social support, all had a positive attitude towards child labour, while market women in monogamous settings, those with education, those living in urban areas as well as those with a high level of social support, all had negative attitudes towards child labour.

## 35. Adisa, Rashid S. and Oluwasegun A. Adekunle

2007, 'Role Duality Among School-Age Children Participating in Farming in Some Villages in Kwara State, Nigeria'. *Africa Development*, Vol. 32, no. 3, pp. 108-120.

This paper examines rural children's role duality as school pupils and farm participants in Edu Local Government Area in Kwara State, Nigeria through a multi-stage cluster random sampling of data from 229 respondents aged between five and sixteen years. The study found that 44 percent of the respondents were simultaneously schooling and farming, while the remaining respondents were either in school or farming. The study also found that no significant difference existed in farm participation levels of respondents attending school and those that were not, while a significant difference in innovation awareness existed in favour of respondents in school. Parental influence, peer group and school farms were also found to be significantly related to respondents' participation in agriculture.

## 36. Admassie, Assefa

2002, 'Explaining the High Incidence of Child Labour in Sub-Saharan Africa', *African Development Review*, Vol. 14, no. 2, pp. 251-275.

This study examines the link between children's labour force participation and some macroeconomic variables using aggregated data from sub-Saharan Africa. The results show that the high incidence of child labour in sub-Saharan Africa can be explained, amongst others, in terms of the high incidence of poverty, the predominance of a poorly developed agricultural sector, high fertility rates leading to high population growth, and low education participation. Contrary to some recent arguments, which have questioned the direct link between poverty and child labour, the results of this study show that poverty is indeed one of the most important reasons for the high incidence of child labour in Africa.

## 37. Alila, Patrick O. and John Murimi Njoka, (eds)

2009, '*Child Labour: New and Enduring Forms From and African Development Policy Perspective*. Nairobi: International Labour Organisation (ILO), IPEC and the Institute for Development Studies (IDS), University of Nairobi (UON). pp. 173.

A publication resulting from an ILO-IPEC supported project on Enhancing capacity for research and teaching on child labour at the Institute for Development Studies, University of Nairobi, Kenya. This collective volume offers a descriptive analysis of child labour as a contemporary global human development problem. It focuses on Kenya.

## 38. Akurang-Parry, Kwabena O.

2002, 'The Loads are Heavier than Usual': Forced Labor by Women and Children in the Central Province, Gold Coast (Colonial Ghana), ca. 1900-2002. *African Economic History*, No. 30, pp. 31-51.

Covering the period 1900-1940, this study shows that female and child forced labour in the Central Province of the Gold Coast (colonial Ghana) contributed immensely to the early 20th-century colonial economy. The evidence suggests that female and child labour, but particularly prepubescent female labour, was prominent in the regions with booming cash crop and export-import economies, as well as in areas where the infrastructure was being built.

## 39. Anarfi, John Kwasi and Stephen O. Kwankye, (eds)

2009, *Independent Migration of Children in Ghana*, Accra: ISSER, University of Ghana.

This edited volume aims to provide insight into internal migration from the northern savannah regions of Ghana to the 'rich' cocoa producing and mineral-extraction south for work that has steadily come to include the independent migration of children. Contributors grapple with various issues related to children migrating for economic reasons and the sociocultural and emotional consequences resulting from such migration.

## 40. Antoine, Philippe, Razafindrakoto, Mireille and Roubaud, François

2001, 'Contraints de Rester Jeunes? Evolution de L'insertion dans Trois Capitales Africaines: Dakar, Yaoundé, Antananarivo', *Autrepart*, Vol. 18, pp. 17-36.

The authors argue that youth in Dakar, Yaoundé and Antananarivo are the victims of a prolonged crisis that engulfed their countries in the 1990s, and forced them to postpone their scheduled entry into adulthood. Compared to their older counterparts these youth access both the first paid job for residential autonomy and family formation much later in their lives. The other key observation is that neither their high levels of education, nor their delayed entry into adulthood allows them to escape deteriorating socioeconomic conditions prevailing in their countries especially when compared to those experienced by their parents at the time of adulthood. Indeed the more educated youth are more vulnerable to these challenges.

## 41. Anugwom, Edlyne E.

2003, 'Child Labour in the Context of Globalisation in Nigeria', *The African Anthropologist*, Vol. 10, no. 2, pp. 105-124.

This paper argues that the incidence of child labour in Nigeria has been heightened by globalization, particularly the economic rationalism underlying it. Globalization, manifested initially in the guise of the adjustment programme in Nigeria in the mid-1980s, has since grown to include the so-called post-adjustment policies of privatisation, deregulation, minimal state role or liberalization.

## 42. Berlan, Amanda

2009, 'Child Labour and Cocoa: Whose Voices Prevail?' *International Journal of Sociology and Social Policy,* Vol. 29, Issue 3, pp. 141-151.

This paper provides ethnographic data on the lives of children working in cocoa-producing communities in Ghana in order to illustrate the importance of contextualisation in understanding the phenomenon of child labour. Based on anthropological fieldwork carried out in Ghana using participant observation and child-focused participatory research methods the author shows that the children involved in this study worked freely and willingly on family cocoa farms. It also shows that research and interventions must be context-based and child-centred as forms of child labour in cocoa are not uniform across West Africa. The author challenges many of the assumptions made about child labour in cocoa and offers new insights into the lives of children in these communities.

## 43. Bhukuth, Augendra

2009, 'Le Travail des Enfants: Limites de la Definition', *Monde en Développement,* Vol. 37, No. 146, pp. 27-32.

The author discusses the conventional definition of child labour especially as outlined by the ILO, which considers a child to be a worker if he/she is under the age of 18 and being economically active meaning that the fruit of his/her labour is directly or indirectly connected to the market. The author considers this definition limiting and argues that it does not always prevail especially in the case of children living and working in the streets.

## 44. Carrier, Neil

2005, "'Miraa' is Cool': the Cultural Importance of 'Miraa' (Khat) for Tigania and Igembe Youth in Kenya', *Journal of African Cultural Studies*, Vol. 17, no. 2, pp. 201-218.

In this paper the author argues that 'Miraa' (khat), grown intensively in the Nyambene Hills district of Kenya by the Tigania and Igembe is of prime economic importance for the region, and Nyambene-grown 'miraa' feeds a growing international, as well as national, market. While it is a controversial substance condemned as a 'drug' by many - Tigania and Igembe have much pride in the substance, emphasizing not just its economic role but also its place in Nyambene traditions. It is linked strongly to Tigania and Igembe ancestors, and its consumption is said to have been once restricted to the elders alone. Author concludes that that 'miraa' is not only a successful commodity but is also linked to the local people's heritage, and helps forge an identity for the youth as as young, modern and Meru.

## 45. Charles, Joseph Okokon and Charles, Arit O.

2004, 'Family and Child Labour: A Study of Child Hawkers in Calabar', *Journal of Social Development in Africa*, Vol. 19, No. 2, pp. 113-133.

The authors discuss hawking as a variant of child labour and examine the relationship between hawking and economic backgrounds of families in Calabar metropolis, Nigeria. Using historical, descriptive and survey research the researchers interviewed 700 child hawkers from the ages 1–16 years in six clusters in Calabar. The study found that, although child labour has a long history in Calabar in particular and Efikland in general, child hawking as a variant of child labour is a product of the tough socioeconomic circumstances that engulfed the last quarter of the twentieth century. Although hawking begins when children are of school age, there is a higher concentration of child hawkers in late primary and early secondary school classes than in early primary and late secondary school classes. Hawking is an ordered and organized activity, which thrives among low-income parents and guardians as a coping strategy. Child hawking is a socialization process, which prepares the child for adult economic life. It provides child-to-child learning and training for skill development. The authors conclude that child hawking becomes exploitative when it attracts stringent negative sanctions; otherwise it is like any other 'child service' to a family that is in need of such assistance.

## 46.    Cockburn, John and Benoit Dostie

2007, 'Child Work and Schooling: The Role of Household Asset Profiles and Poverty in Rural Ethiopia', *Journal of African Economies*, Vol. 16, no. 4, pp. 519-563.

The authors extend the theoretical and empirical framework to better address demand determinants for child labour using rural Ethiopia as a case study and argue that this demand is household-specific given that in Ethiopia child labour is overwhelmingly performed for the child's own household in the absence of a smoothly functioning child labour market. The results suggest that the demand for child labour plays a major role in child time-use decisions and that this demand varies between households according to their asset profiles and household composition. In addition, by adequately addressing the demand side, the authors actually find support for a poverty-child labour link.

## 47.    Dijk, Diana van and Francien van Driel

2009, 'Supporting Child-Headed Households in South Africa: Whose Best Interests?' *Journal of Southern African Studies*, Vol. 35, no. 4, pp. 915-927.

This article examines assumptions about the provision of support for children and young people in child-headed households in sub-Saharan Africa. The example of South Africa is used to assess appropriate family- and community-based support and assistance. The South African Children's Act of 2007 proposes that child-headed households should be supported by an adult mentor, who will act in the children and young people's best interests. However, qualitative research among child-headed households in Port Elizabeth shows that so-called 'adult support' mostly does not contribute to children and young people's well-being. Children and young people often are not consulted about care arrangements, are not taken seriously, or are even worse off after adult interventions, resulting in many having a sense of powerlessness over their situation. An emphasis on access to social grants increases the potential for abuse of these youngsters. The study reveals the value of taking generational constructions into account in assessing current practice and developing more appropriate support arrangements.

## 48.  Garcia, Marito and Jean Fares, (eds)

2008, *Youth in Africa's labor market*, Washington, DC: World Bank.

This book examines the challenges African youth face in their transition to work and presents a strategy for meeting these challenges. It argues that African youth start working too early and are unprepared to meet the demands of the labour market, limiting their contribution to economic growth and increasing their vulnerability to poverty and economic hardship. The book describes how Africa's young people spend their time and presents a case for investing in youth in Africa, analysing the two paths to working life for Africa's youth: directly (without the benefit of education) and through school. It also presents new evidence on the effects of education on employment and income in selected countries, and examines youth unemployment and its determinants.

## 49.  Grier, Beverly

2004, 'Child Labor and Africanist Scholarship: a Critical Overview', *African Studies Review*, Vol. 47, no. 2, pp. 1-25.

The essay critically reviews the extant scholarly literature on children and work in the precolonial, colonial, and postcolonial periods and concludes that child labour is either underresearched or undertheorized to the detriment of our understanding of gender, patriarchy, agency, the formation of worker and political consciousness, capital accumulation, and the State. The essay argues that children have shaped and continue to shape history in Africa and that childhood is a terrain of struggle in which numerous social and political forces (including children, patriarchy, capital, and the State) seek constructions that suit their particular (and changing) interests.

## 50. Issa, A.O. and K.I.N. Nwalo

2008, 'Factors Affecting the Career Choice of Undergraduates in Nigerian Library and Information Science Schools', *African Journal of Library, Archives & Information Science*, Vol. 18, no. 1, pp. 23-31.

This study investigates the low preference for library and information science as a first-choice course of study by the undergraduates of Nigerian library schools. The survey research design was adopted, with the Career Choice Influence Questionnaire, as the main data collection instrument. In all, 1,228 students from eight Nigerian university library schools participated in the study. The study revealed that for the majority of the students LIS was not their first choice, but that they ended up in the library school as a last resort. The study concludes that despite the evidence of improved popularity of the LIS programme among the respondents, it remains largely unpopular among prospective undergraduates in Nigeria when compared with other courses such as accountancy, medicine and law.

## 51. Jacquemin, M•lanie

2006, ÒCan The Language of Rights Get Hold of The Complex Realities of Child Domestic Work? The Case of Young Domestic Workers in Abidjan, Ivory Coast,Ó *Childhood. A Global Journal of Child Research*, Vol. 13, No. 3, pp. 389-406.

This review examines refractions of children's rights in development practice from an anthropological point of view and considers the case of young domestic girls working in Abidjan. The author argues that child labour legislation and the children's rights perspective in Abidjan is permeated by patriarchal values that mask the exploitation of work performed in the domestic arena under the cover of (pseudo) kinship ties. The author contends that development programmes that target young domestic servants in a children's rights-framed approach risk obscuring situations where children are put to work and actually exploited.

## 52. Kidolezi, Yohanne N., Jessica A. Holmes, Hugo Ñopo, and Paul M. Sommers

2007, 'Selection and Reporting Bias in Household Surveys of Child Labor: Evidence from Tanzania', *African Development Review*, Vol. 19, no. 2, pp. 368-378.

In this paper, the authors compare the demographic and labour market characteristics of children working in the street obtained from the 2000 Tanzanian Integrated Labour Force Survey, a government-sponsored household survey, with the results obtained in a 2004 survey of children who work in the street in the city of Mwanza in northern Tanzania. The study in Mwanza finds that 17.2 percent of working street children do not belong to households and further, that these children are significantly different from those who reside in formal households.

## 53. Kea, Pamela

2007, 'Girl Farm Labour and Double-Shift Schooling in the Gambia: The Paradox of Development I', *Canadian Journal of African Studies*, Vol. 41, no. 2, pp. 258-288.

This article examines the intensification of Gambian girls' domestic and farm labour contributions as a result of the introduction of double-shift schooling, drawing on fieldwork among female farmers and their daughters in Brikama, Western Division, in 1996/1997 and 2005. The article argues that double-shift schooling facilitates the intensification and increased appropriation of surplus value from girls' household and farm labour because girls are more readily able to meet gendered labour obligations that are central to the moral economy of the household and to the demands of agrarian production; second, double-shift schooling highlights the paradoxical nature of development intervention where, on the one hand, legislation and policy call for a reduction in child labour by increasing access to school and, on the other, neoliberal educational policy serves to facilitate the intensification of girls' domestic and farm labour.

## 54.   Levine, S.L.

2006, 'The 'Picaninny Wage': an Historical Overview of the Persistence of Structural Inequality and Child Labour in South Africa', *Anthropology Southern Africa*, Vol. 29, no. 3/4, pp. 122-131.

This paper considers the recruitment of children and youths in colonial and postcolonial South Africa, exploring the early legislation that transformed the nature of childhood in pre-colonial South Africa, and contributes to emerging scholarship on social constructions of childhood. The paper draws attention to historical shifts and continuities in the nature of child labour, and in relation to economic exploitation, racial oppression and childhood agency. Spanning the eras of pre-colonial relations of production, child slavery in the 1600s, and children's work under colonial rule in the mining, domestic service, and agricultural industries, the paper considers the differential configurations of the labour demands of children. Working against the tendency to regard child labour as a sentimental human rights issue, the paper provides a critical perspective against which to focus on contemporary debates about the rights of children in post-apartheid South Africa, and redress the participation of children in processes of total social reproduction.

## 55.   Lokshin, Michael M. Elena Glinskaya and Marito Garcia

2004, 'The effect of Early Childhood Development Programmes on Womens Labour Force Participation and Older Childrens Schooling in Kenya', *Journal of African economies*, Vol. 13, no. 2, pp. 240-276.

The authors analyse the effect of childcare costs on households behaviour in Kenya. The research is based on data from the 1994 Kenya Welfare Monitoring Survey (WMS II) and the 1995 Kenya Early Childhood Development Centres Survey (KECDCS). For households with children 3-7 years of age, the authors model the participation of the mother in paid work, the participation of other household members in paid work, household demand for schooling for school-aged children and household demand for child care. They find that high costs of childcare discourage households from using formal childcare and reduce the level of mothers participation in market work.

## 56.  Manzo, Kate

2005, 'Modern slavery, Global Capitalism & Deproletarianisation in West Africa', *Review of African Political Economy*. Vol. 32, no. 106, p. 521-534.

This paper explores the concept of 'new' or modern slavery in the wake of media reports of widespread child slavery on cocoa plantations in Côte d'Ivoire (the RCI). The first part defines slavery as unpaid forced labour, identifies the defining feature of modern slavery as the shift in the master-slave relation from legal ownership to illegal control, and then draws on a range of secondary sources to show that child slavery does exist in the Côte d'Ivoire even if numbers are contested. The many thousands of child slaves apparently trafficked from Mali make this a West African (and not simply Ivorian) phenomenon. The aspects of global capitalist development used in part two to explain the Ivorian situation, namely deproletarianization and the costs of adjustment are also wider processes not unique to one country.

## 57.  Mukamugambira, Pascasie and Kwaku Osei-Hwedie

2007, 'Factors Influencing Attitudes of Botswana Youth Towards Manual Work: Implications for Employment', *Journal of Social Development in Africa*, Vol. 22, no. 2, pp. 107-135.

This paper examines attitudes of youth towards manual work, factors that contributed to these attitudes, and the implications of these attitudes for youth employment. It is based on a study of 119 youths, aged 15 to 29 years, working in the construction, domestic and farming sectors in Gaborone (Botswana) and three neighbouring villages. The paper concludes that, generally, youth in Botswana demonstrate positive attitudes towards manual work. Factors influencing youth attitudes to manual work include: the importance attached to work; gender, age and level of education; the intrinsic value of manual work; and perceived usefulness of manual work by youth, employers and society in general. The need to support their families, a desire to secure steady employment and financial self-reliance are other factors that motivate youth to do manual work.

## 58. Mukherjee, Jaydeep

2008, 'Child Labour, Education, Participation and Economic Growth in Sub-Saharan Africa: an Empirical Study', *Research Review: Institute of African Studies*, Vol. 24, no. 1, pp. 53-70.

This study examines the interaction between child labour, primary school participation and per capita economic growth for Sub-Saharan Africa in a holistic framework using a two-stage least squares (2SLS) regression model and dummy variables to capture the regional and income classifications. The results show that per capita GDP growth rate, public expenditure on education as percentage of GDP, net primary enrollment ratio and percentage of children reaching grade 5 in school are inversely related with the incidence of children's labour force participation, while total fertility rate which reflects population growth, is positively related with child labour.

## 59. Muzvidziwa, Victor Ngonidzashe

2006, 'Child Labour or Child Work?: Whither Policy', *Research Review: Institute of African Studies*, Vol. 22, no. 1, pp. 23-33.

Based on anthropological research on working children in Zimbabwe, the argument presented in this paper is not whether or not children should work, for the focus should rather be on the conditions under which they work. Often, in poor countries children have to work as a survival strategy. The role of children in poor households demands that they work as a way to ensure household survival. The problematic of child work has policy implications and is something that poor countries need to address taking their specific situations into account instead of embracing policies based on Northern definitions, perceptions and notions of childhood. The author concludes that child work can be seen as a legitimate activity and an acceptable face of poverty in poor countries.

## 60. Ray, Ranjan

2002, 'The Determinants of Child Labour and Child Schooling in Ghana', *Journal of African Economies*, Vol. 11, no. 4, pp. 561-590.

This paper investigates the main determinants of child labour and child schooling in Ghana, with special reference to their interaction. The empirical results contain some evidence of sharp rural urban differences, thus pointing to the need to adopt region specific policies in enhancing child welfare.

## 61.  Scheld, Suzanne

2007, 'Youth Cosmopolitanism: Clothing, the City and Globalization in Dakar, Senegal', *City & Society*, Volume 19. Issue 2, pp. 232 - 253)

This research is based on fieldwork conducted in Dakar and New York City between 1996 and 2005. Research methods include interviews, participant observation, focus groups and engaging youth in authoring informal fashion magazines which feature their own photography and stories about contemporary clothing trends in Dakar. It shows how Dakarois youth use dress to shape the city and urban identity despite the declining economy and for many, extreme poverty. The author also shows that because the informal economy is intensely competitive for both buyers and sellers, youth rely on social networks, various forms of reciprocity, and trust in order to perform their work.

## 62.  Tarinyeba, Winifred M.

2007, 'Poverty, Trade and Child Labour in the Developing World: an Analysis of Efforts to Combat Child Labour in Uganda', *East African Journal of Peace & Human Rights*, Vol. 13, no. 2, pp. 294-308.

This paper examines the problem of child labour (with special attention for Uganda) from three perspectives: poverty, HIV/AIDS and global trade. It involves an analysis of empirical and theoretical literature on poverty, trade and child labour. The paper specifically focuses on the economic outcomes of a global trading system managed by the World Trade Organization (WTO) that inherently disadvantages poor countries and its implications for child labour.

## 63.  Togunde, Dimeji and Sarah Richardson

2006, 'Household Size and Composition as Correlates of Child Labour in Urban Nigeria', *Africa Development*, Vol. 31, no. 1, pp. 50-65.

This paper draws on interviews with 1,535 parents and their children to examine the relationship between child labour and various household variables in urban Nigeria, where child labour studies have been very limited. The authors provide a comprehensive overview of the household factors and residential dynamics through which child labour evolves. Research findings demonstrate that although child labour is mostly caused by poverty and the need to prepare children with skills and training useful for future occupations, the size of the household, number of children in the household, number of children contributing to the household income, child's age, and age at which child started working are all significantly and positively correlated with children's hours of work.

## 64.   Zhou, Honest

2002, 'Determinants of youth earnings: The Case of Harare', *Zambezia*, Vol. 29, no. 2, pp. 213-220.

This paper investigates the factors that are important in determining youth earnings in the formal sector in Harare, Zimbabwe. It uses a sample cohort of 660 21-year olds employed in the formal sector, who were observed in 1996. The theoretical approach adopted is that of human capital theory. The survey collected information on the individuals' earnings, employment history, education, occupation and training as well as socioeconomic characteristics, including gender. The results suggest that human capital variables are important determinants of youth earnings in the formal sector. Such variables include the number of years spent in education, the highest level of education achieved and the choice of subjects at GCE 'O' level.

# Part III

## Children's Rights

## 65. Adeleke, F.A.R.

2008, 'Critical Appraisal of the Offence of Rape Under the codes and the new Child Right Act 2003', *Journal of Oriental and African Studies,* Vol. 17, pp. 185-197.

The present paper shows the inherent fallacy in the present law outlined in section 357 of the Nigeria Criminal Code by bringing into focus the possibility and incidents of rape of men by women. The author argues that events in society have rendered fallacious the philosophical reasoning that there is a permanent implied consent from a wife to sexual intercourse at all times with her husband and examines the new definition of rape as contained in the new Child Right Act of 2003. The paper brings into focus the inconsistency of the offence of rape with the express provision of the Constitution and the need to redefine rape in line with societal reality and what obtains in other jurisdictions.

## 66. Archambault, Caroline

2009, 'Pain with Punishment and the Negotiation of Childhood: an Ethnographic Analysis of Children's Rights Processes in Maasailand', *Africa: Journal of the International African Institute,* Vol. 79, no. 2, pp. 282-302.

This article provides an ethnographic analysis of the practice of corporal punishment among the Maasai in domestic and primary school settings, exploring its pedagogical, developmental and social significance, and illuminating its role in the production and negotiation of identities and personhood. The author shows the pull between on the one hand Children's rights activists who contend that corporal punishment in schools is a form of child abuse which hinders children's learning and on the other hand most parents and teachers in Maasailand, Kenya, who consider corporal punishment, if properly employed, to be one of the most effective ways to instill the discipline necessary for children to learn and grow well.

## 67. Cassim, Fawzia

2003, 'The Rights of Child Witnesses Versus the Accused's Right to Confrontation: a Comparative Perspective', *The Comparative and International Law Journal of Southern Africa*, Vol. 36, no. 1, pp. 65-82.

This article examines the question of whether the rights of child victims of sexual assault take precedence over the confrontation rights of the accused. Protective measures for child victims in South Africa and in foreign systems, such as the United States of America, Canada, United Kingdom and Australia, are examined. The examination reveals that the right to confrontation is not absolute. In exceptional circumstances, the accused's right to confrontation will yield to the greater public interest in protecting the rights of vulnerable child witnesses. The article recommends the development of alternative legal measures to achieve a balance between these competing interests.

## 68. Church, Joan

2003, 'Children: Some Perspectives on their Legal Position and the Development of Indigenous Law', *Anthropology Southern Africa*, Vol. 26, no. 3/4, pp. 119-123.

This article considers the position of children in South Africa under the new constitutional dispensation, as seen in comparative perspective and in the light of present and proposed legislation and of indigenous law. This is done with a view to possible legal reform in the private and public domain. The article discusses relevant case law and suggests that the development of indigenous law might be effected in accordance with the concept of 'ubuntu' and the values entrenched in the Republic of South Africa Constitution Act 108 of 1996. 'Ubuntu' is seen as including, amongst others, the idea of group solidarity and the interdependence of members within the group.

## 69. Clark, Brigitte

2002, 'From Rights to Responsibilities?: an Overview of Recent Developments Relating to the Parent/child Relationship in South African Common Law', The *Comparative and International Law Journal of Southern Africa*, Vol. 35, no. 2, pp. 216-235.

This article examines the parent/child relationship in South African law in the light of recent legal developments in this country. It further assesses the influence of international conventions and the constitutionalization of children's rights on South African jurisprudence in this regard. The article further places the developments in South African child law within an international context with particular reference to developments in the law relating to parental authority and guardianship and developments in the law relating to corporal punishment and domestic violence. Children's rights to autonomy in medical decision-making are also analysed with special reference to recent proposals for changes by the South African Law Commission in its Review of the Child Care Act. The article includes some discussion of the position of extra-martial children and their relationship with their parents and concludes with a brief discussion of the socioeconomic rights of many poverty-stricken children in South Africa, especially those who will be affected by the HIV/AIDS pandemic for whom there may well be no-one who assumes the role of parent.

## 70.  Dawes, Andrew, Rachel Bray and Amelia van der Merwe, (eds)

2007, *Monitoring Child Well-Being: a South African Rights-Based Approach.* Cape Town: HSRC.

This book provides a practical, user-friendly approach to monitoring the well-being of children in South Africa. Its ideological base is the child-rights focus in the South African Constitution, the UN Convention on the Rights of the Child and the African Charter on the Rights and Welfare of Children. It is divided into two main parts. Part One, Rationales for Indicator Development, provides the conceptual foundations which inform the development of the rights-based approach to monitoring child well-being, touching upon such topics as child poverty, child survival and health care, with a special emphasis on HIV/AIDS, early childhood development and education, and child protection. Part Two contains comprehensive tables of indicators for the topics covered in Part One, with recommended measurement and data sources.

## 71.   De Waal, Alex and Nicolas Argenti, (eds)

2002, *Young Africa: Realising the Rights of Children and Youth,* Trenton, NJ: Africa World Press.

This edited volume covers papers presented at the Pan African Forum on the Future of Children in Africa, held in Cairo in May 2001, with the purpose of formulating and adopting the ´African Common Position´ on the rights of the child in Africa in preparation for the upcoming UN General Assembly Special Session on Children. Contributions cover various topics such as Child survival and development, education, militarism, Pentecostal Christianity and the Rights of the Child in Africa.

## 72.   Du Plessis, Max

2004, 'Children Under International Criminal Law', *African Security Review,* Vol. 13, no. 2, pp. 103-111.

This paper outlines the norms that exist, both under human rights law and humanitarian law, in respect of children who are caught up, whether as civilians or combatants, in armed conflict. The paper pays particular attention to the role of the International Criminal Court in this respect, and uses the first ever judgement regarding recruitment of child soldiers handed down by the Special Court for Sierra Leone, on 31 May 2004, as a case study.

## 73.   Kaime, Thoko

2009/10, 'The foundations of rights in the African Charter on the Rights and Welfare of the Child: a Historical and Philosophical Account', *African Journal of Legal Studies,* Vol. 3, no. 1, pp. 119-136.

This article examines the culturally-based critiques of the international human rights paradigm generally and children's rights in particular, with specific reference to Africa. In this regard, the paper identifies gaps in the analyses of the African Charter on the Rights and Welfare of the Child and analyses the documents and literature that focus on the rights and welfare of the child. The author raises several important questions regarding the propriety of this special category of human rights in the African context.

## 74. Kassan, Daksha

2008, 'The Protection of Children from All Forms of Violence — African Experiences'. In *Children's Rights in Africa: A Legal Perspective*, edited by Julia Sloth-Nielsen, Hamphire, England: Ashgate Publishing Limited, pp. 165-81.

This chapter examines what the concept of violence entails in the context of Africa, discusses applicable provisions in international and regional instruments, sketches the situation in Africa, and provides some examples of ways in which specific African countries have sought to address certain issues relating to violence against children. Author notes that while many African countries have ratified various children's rights documents the diversity of cultures and legal systems in the continent renders some of the expected human rights protocols untenable. This leads to children being subjected to various forms of violence and abuse even and especially by their caregivers.

## 75. Khamasi, Wanjiku

2009, 'Post Female Circumcision: a Call for Collective Unmasking', *East African Journal of Peace & Human Rights*, Vol. 15, no. 1, pp. 158-170.

This paper, which advocates the banning of female circumcision, is informed by three theories, namely the standpoint theory, philosophical hermeneutics and the feminist theory, as well as by the author's lived experiences. It argues that Kenya's government banned female circumcision for girls under 18 years through the 2001 Children's Act, privileges the voices of the uncircumcised, thereby, unfortunately, reinforcing 'otherness' and suggests a conceptual model to move forward in the matter based on what bell hooks refers to as conversation, dedication to truth and collective unmasking.

## 76. Lloyd, Amanda

2002, 'A Theoretical Analysis of the Reality of Children's Rights in Africa: an Introduction to the African Charter on the Rights and Welfare of the Child', *African Human Rights Law Journal*, Vol. 2, no. 1, pp. 11-32.

The author analyzes the African Charter on the Rights and Welfare of the Child that was adopted at the OAU Assembly held at Addis Ababa,

Ethiopia, in July 1990 and ratified by fifteen member States of the OAU in 1999, arguing that it does not impose a Western conception on Africa but promotes a modernized Africa. Showing that in modern African states, children can no longer be regarded as property, there is an urgent need for a better understanding of children's needs and rights especially when children from the age of fifteen are considered to be eligible for recruitment into armed forces.

## 77. Mezmur, Benyam D.

2008, "As painful as Giving Birth': a Reflection on the Madonna Adoption Saga', *The Comparative and International Law Journal of Southern Africa*, Vol. 41, no. 3, pp. 383-403.

This article comments on the decision of the High Court of Malawi handed down on 28 May 2008 in the matter of the Adoption of Children Act (CAP 26:01) and in the matter of David Banda (a male infant), or 'the Madonna judgment'. This is discussed in the context of the Convention on the Rights of the Child and the African Charter on the Rights and Welfare of the Child. The article examines a range of issues such as the status of inter-country adoption in international law, the principle of the best interests of the child, the role of culture, the right to privacy, and the child's participation. It concludes that the implications of the case are far-reaching and predominantly positive.

## 78. Mezmur, Benyam D.

2007, 'Still an Infant or Now a Toddler? : the Work of the African Committee of Experts on the Rights and Welfare of the Child and its 8th Ordinary Session', *African Human Rights Law Journal*, Vol. 7, no. 1, pp. 258-275.

This article focuses on the 8th ordinary meeting, initially planned for May 2006 but eventually held from 27 November to 1 December 2006 in Addis Ababa. Among the topics on the agenda were the draft guidelines for the consideration of communications, for the conducting of investigations and the criteria for granting observer status with the Committee. The author concludes that while the Committee's weak start, the lack of adequate resources for its effective functioning, and a lack of interest on the part of member-States of the African Union in meeting their obligations, particularly with regard to State reporting, still continue to prevent the African Children's Committee from maximizing its potential, there are nevertheless abundant signs of improvement.

## 79.    Mezmur, Benyam D.

2006, 'The African Committee of Experts on the Rights and Welfare of the Child: an Update', *African Human Rights Law Journal*, Vol. 6, no. 2, pp. 549-571.

The present article is an update on recent developments and activities of the Children's Committee. Focus is on the work it has undertaken from the time of its 5th meeting in Nairobi, Kenya (8 to 12 November 2004) up to its 7th meeting in Addis Ababa, Ethiopia (19-21 December 2005). It covers new committee members, the establishment of a secretariat, the role played by the Children's Committee in the monitoring and implementation of the provisions of the African Children's Charter (State reporting, consideration of communications, fact-finding mission to Northern Uganda), promotional activities, and the link between the Children's Committee and partners, donors and civil society.

## 80.    Mezmur, Benyam D. and Julia Sloth-Nielsen

2008', An Ice-breaker: State Party Reports and the 11th session of the African Committee of Experts on the Rights and Welfare of the Child', *African Human Rights Law Journal*, Vol. 8, no. 2, pp. 596-616.

This paper highlights the work of the African Committee of Experts on the Rights and Welfare of the Child during the May 2008 session. While little attention is paid to the proceedings of the 11th session, partly as a result of the fact that the session was short-lived (only three days, composed of open and closed sessions), the procedures for the Pre-Session, as well as the substance of the four reports that were discussed during the Pre-Session (from Egypt, Mauritius, Nigeria and Rwanda), occupy centre stage. In conclusion, it is argued that the whole exercise of the Pre-Session was an ice-breaker and represents progress in its own right.

## 81.   O'Neal, Nicole

2008, 'Corporal Punishment in Public Schools: a Call for Legal Reform', *African Human Rights Law Journal*, Vol. 8, no. 1, pp. 60-78.

This article explains how laws authorizing public school corporal punishment breach human rights law, and calls for law reform in African States. In addition to the repeal of such laws, this article suggests legislation that could be implemented domestically to condemn and prohibit this practice.

## 82.   Rosa, Solange and Mira Dutschke

2006, 'Child Rights at the Core: the Use of International Law in South African Cases on Children's Socio-Economic Rights', *South African Journal on Human Rights*, Vol. 22, pt. 2, pp. 224-260.

This article argues that the courts have an essential role to play in the realization of international human rights law. Analysis of the judgments of the South African courts shows, however, that there are flaws in their use and enforcement of international and regional human rights law. It is argued that the courts' judgments on socioeconomic rights have not properly defined the scope and content of children's socioeconomic rights in the Bill of Rights. Recommendations are made as to how the courts should strengthen their role in promoting the socioeconomic rights of children through the considered use and enforcement of international law.

## 83.   Skelton, Ann

2009, 'The development of a Fledgling Child Rights Jurisprudence in Eastern and Southern Africa Based on International and Regional Instruments', *African Human Rights Law Journal*, Vol. 9, no. 2, pp. 482-500.

This article charts the development of a child law jurisprudence that is emerging in Eastern and Southern Africa and records how judgments are beginning to make reference to the United Nations Convention on the Rights of the Child and the African Charter on the Rights and Welfare of the Child, and even to less prominent instruments such as the Hague Convention on the Protection of Children and Co-operation in Respect of Inter-Country Adoption (1993) and the Hague Convention on Civil Aspects of International Child Abduction. Attention is paid to certain textual differences between the UN Convention and the African Children's Charter, and the extent to which these discrepancies have played a role in the development of child law jurisprudence that might be described as uniquely African. The article concludes that there is evidence of the beginnings of a specifically African jurisprudence in child law. It is noted, however, that more can be done to promote children's legal rights in the region through the ratification by more African countries of the Hague Conventions, and also through courts in the Eastern and Southern African region taking note of each other's jurisprudence.

## 84.   Sloth-Nielsen, Julia, (ed.)

2008, *Children's Rights in Africa: a Legal Perspective*, Burlington, VT: Ashgate.

This collection is anchored in an African conception of children's rights and the law, and reflects contemporary discourses taking place in the region in the children's rights sphere. The central objective is to profile recent developments and experiences in furthering children's legal rights in Africa. The chapters in Part 1 are general in nature, and discuss the regional system of protection of human rights and children's rights in Africa and Part 2 highlights child participation in African law reform processes, restorative justice and children's rights, the protection of refugee children, children with disabilities and the right to education, and child labour.

## 85.   Sloth-Nielsen, Julia

2008, 'Realising Childrern's Rights to Legal Representation and to be Heard in Judicial Proceedings: an Update', *South African Journal on Human Rights*, Vol. 24, pt. 3, pp. 495-524.

This article charts some key developments in law, policy and implementation that constitute such practices. The article also argues that apart from merely serving as the child's voice in the courtroom setting, effective child lawyering is additionally contingent on a commitment to seeking out children in need of services, an emphasis more broadly on stakeholder relationships in the sector, and a willingness to adjust to changing circumstances.

## 86.  Sloth-Nielsen, Julia

2008, 'Win Some, Lose Some: the 10th Ordinary Session of the African Committee of Experts on the Rights and Welfare of the Child', In: *African Human Rights Law Journal*, Vol. 8, no. 1, pp. 207-220.

This discussion highlights the inertia of the African Committee of Experts on the Rights and Welfare of the Child, the monitoring body of the African Charter on the Rights and Welfare of the Child, held its 10th ordinary session in October 2007, exemplifying its failure to examine any of the State reports submitted to it. Some cause for optimism may be derived from the appointment of a permanent Secretary to the Committee.

## 87.  Sloth-Nielsen, J. and Benyam D. Mezmur

2008, 'A dutiful Child: the Implications of Article 31 of the African Children's Charter', *Journal of African Law*, Vol. 52, no. 2, pp. 159-189.

After setting the platform for discussion by highlighting international experiences and outlining the African concept of human rights, this article critically examines and attempts to clarify the precise meaning, content, conditions of compliance and application of those duties for children. By way of conclusion, it suggests that article 31 represents a valuable addition to the international human rights agenda, and that a purposeful interpretation of its constituent parts reveals that children should be required to play a role at family, community, national and continental levels, in accordance with their age and maturity as they grow up, as part and parcel of their heritage, empowerment and developing citizenship.

## 88.  Sloth-Nielsen, Julia and Benyam D. Mezmur

2009, 'Out of the Starting Blocks: the 12th and 13th Sessions of the African Committee of Experts on the Rights and Welfare of the Child', *African Human Rights Law Journal*, Vol. 9, no. 1, pp. 336-352.

Reports on the 12th and 13th meetings of the African Children's Committee held in November 2008 and April 2009 respectively and highlights the consideration of the first country reports to the African Committee, the benefits of a regionally-specific child rights treaty and the formal grouping of civil society organizations and individuals dedicated to furthering the regional influence of the African Children's Charter.

## 89.   Sloth-Nielsen, Julia and Benyam D. Mezmur

2007, 'Surveying the Research Landscape to Promote Children's Legal Rights in an African Context', *African Human Rights Law Journal*, Vol. 7, no. 2, pp. 330-353.

This article identifies research themes and topics of special relevance to the furtherance of children's rights in the context of Africa in order to sharpen and strengthen the capacity to promote good practice and promising solutions. The article surveys an array of possibilities for research to promote the implementation of children's rights in an African context. It explores issues including assessing law reform processes in support of child rights in an African context; mainstreaming rights-based approaches in general legal frameworks; strengths and weaknesses in legal approaches to children's rights issues; culture, customary law and children's rights; socioeconomic rights; strategies for enhancing child participation in legal and policy processes; the role of the judiciary, courts and national monitoring mechanisms; and regional mechanisms and children's rights. The article incorporates information from a number of different African jurisdictions, comparing and contrasting efforts at child reform in respect of children's rights.

## 90.   Stewart, Linda

2008, 'Interpreting and Limiting the Basic Socio-Economic Rights of Children in Cases Where they Overlap with the Socio-Economic Rights of Others', *South African Journal on Human Rights*, Vol. 24, pt. 3, pp. 472-494.

This article investigates the approach of the Constitutional Court in the interpretation and limitation of the basic socioeconomic rights of children under parental care and suggests an approach that is based on the substantive content of children's socioeconomic rights by applying the two-stage approach of constitutional analysis of the Bill of Rights.

## 91.   Swart, Sarah

2009, 'Unaccompanied Minor Refugees and the Protection of their socioeconomic Rights under Human Rights Law', *African Human Rights Law Journal*, Vol. 9, no. 1, pp. 103-128.

This paper reflects the results of a study whose main objective was to investigate the practical treatment of unaccompanied minor refugees in Ghana and South Africa, and to explore whether such treatment is in accordance with existing international norms and standards for the protection of refugee children. The study focused on the realization of children's socioeconomic rights in order to measure treatment. The paper addresses the obstacles which prevent the proper treatment of unaccompanied minor refugees, and makes recommendations as to how the international community can better regulate the treatment of unaccompanied minor refugees. Through the case studies of Ghana and South Africa, the paper shows that unaccompanied minor refugees are, to a certain extent, lost in the system.

## 92.   Tabaro, Edgar

2008, 'Lost innocence, Shattered Dreams: Child Rights and the Plight of Child Soldiers in Northern Uganda', *Journal of African and International Law*, Vol. 1, no. 3, pp. 87-106.

This paper examines the reasons for the recruitment/use of children in armed conflict; the psychosocial impact of the war on children; sociocultural factors shaping the recruitment of child soldiers; factors related to myth, witchcraft and metaphysics influencing the recruitment of children; the position of children in the Geneva Conventions, humanitarian law and international child human rights law. The paper attributes the failure of international law and the international community in providing protection to children largely to the vague international law regime and the absence of political will among State actors.

## 93.   Tamale, Sylvia

2001, 'How Old is Old Enough?: Defilement Law and the Age of Consent in Uganda', *East African Journal of Peace & Human Rights*, Vol. 7, no. 1, pp. 82-100.

This paper is a product of a two month-research undertaken in April and May 1999 on the debate surrounding the issue of age and sexual consent in Uganda. The research reveals a clear general division within the population. Standing on one side of the divide are religious leaders, women's rights activists, children's advocacy groups, health workers and the urban elite. This group expresses outrage at the suggestion of lowering the age of consent and perceives it as a regression to moral degeneration and a victory for rapists and child abusers. On the other side are judges and magistrates, the police, prosecutors and the rural masses. This group argues for a reduction in the age of consent on the ground that it is more reflective of existing social-cultural realities on the ground.

## 94. Tibatemwa-Ekirikubinza, Lillian

2003, 'Understanding Children's Rights: The Case of Corporal Punishment in Rural Uganda', *East African Journal of Peace and Human Rights*, Vol. 9, no. 1, pp. 115-143.

This paper is based on an empirical pilot study, carried out in 2001 in Nabitende subcounty, a rural community in Iganga District, southeastern Uganda, of the use of corporal punishment in disciplining children at home as well as at school. Interviews were held with parents, teachers, elderly members of society, and student leaders, and focus group discussions were held with students aged 14-17 years. The students and teachers were from two secondary schools. The purpose of the research was to investigate the significance of the Ugandan cultural and social context in the recognition and enforcement of children's rights. This was done within the framework of the minimum standards set out in the United Nations Convention on the Rights of the Child (CRC0), the African Charter for the Rights and Welfare of the Child, Uganda's 1995 Constitution, and the 1996 Children Statute.

## 95. Vincent, Louise

2008, 'Cutting Tradition: the Political Regulation of Traditional Circumcision Rites in South Africa's Liberal Democratic Order', *Journal of Southern African Studies*, Vol. 34, no. 1, pp. 77-91.

This article examines how conflicting conceptions of authority and order regarding male circumcision rites in South Africa have played themselves out with regard to traditional circumcision in South Africa. The author reports on the publicly noted deaths of males undergoing circumcision and how the State has responded by putting in place a variety of mechanisms to regulate the practice, most recently in the form of the 2005 Children's Bill which gives male children the right to refuse circumcision and makes those who circumcise a child against his will guilty of an offence punishable by imprisonment. These attempts by the State to regulate traditional practices have been met with outrage and resistance in some quarters as rituals are commonly identified as mechanisms contributing to social order, maintaining the organization of groups into hierarchies, specifying the performance of roles linked to factors such as age and gender, renewing group unity and a means for the transmission of values across generations.

## 96.   Vrancken, Patrick and Kasturi Chetty

2009, 'International Child Sex Tourism: a South African Perspective', *Journal of African Law*, Vol. 53, no. 1, pp. 111-141.

After explaining the nature and extent of the problem of child sex tourism, this article identifies the relevant instruments of international law, before discussing the legal tools available in South Africa to deal with this issue. South Africa is bound by most of the relevant international instruments and Parliament has also enacted, or is in the process of enacting, a wide range of far-reaching legislative tools.

# Part IV

## Disabilities

## 97. Shumba, Almon and Ethel Taukobong

2009, 'An Evaluation of Policies and Programmes Related to Children with Disabilities in Botswana', *Africa Education Review*, Vol. 6, no. 1, pp. 123-139.

This study seeks to identify available programmes of education and policies that are aimed at helping children with disabilities in schools; determine the nature of services that are available to disabled children in schools; and determine some strategies that the government and society can use to help children with disabilities in Botswana schools. The study found that there are too few schools, and inadequate facilities, for children with disabilities in Botswana.

## 98. Nyirinkindi, Laura

2006, 'A Critical Analysis of Paradigms and Rights in Disability Discourses', *East African Journal of Peace & Human Rights*, Vol. 12, no. 1, pp. 49-64.

The author analyses the role of human rights law and advocacy in setting standards for the quality of education services to make the right to basic education a reality for children with disabilities (CWDs) in Uganda. She focuses on the plight of CWDs under Uganda's current educational curriculum. These children are doubly marginalized as children and as persons with disabilities (PWDs). The author analyses the conceptualization of 'disability' in different disability models - charitable, medical, human rights and social models. She argues that the categorization in the educational curriculum of special needs as 'difficulties', 'impairment', 'disability', and 'retardation' perpetuates victimization and discrimination of CWDs. She concludes that segregation of CWDs from the mainstream schools bars their full inclusion and participation.

## 99. Thomas, Kevin J. A.

2004, 'Disability Among the Children of Migrants in Africa', *African Population Studies*, Vol. 19, suppl. B, pp. 139-164.

This study describes the relationship between child disability and parental migration status in South Africa. Child disability is an important health status indicator that can provide insights into the morbidity levels of migrants in their host societies. The analysis is based on data from the 1996 South African Population Census. The results indicate that though children of immigrants were generally less likely to be disabled than those of the native-born population, the immigrant advantage was significant only among children of immigrants from countries that are not part of the SADC.

## 100. Wright, Fred Lubben and Mac Bain Mkandawire

2007, 'Young Malawians on the Interaction Between Mental Health and HIV/AIDS', *African Journal of AIDS Research*, Vol. 6, no. 3, pp. 297-304.

This study surveys adolescents in southern Malawi on their experience of the impacts of living with HIV or AIDS on one's mental health. At the same time, the study explores the link between mental health problems and subsequent HIV-risk behaviour. Short texts relating everyday scenarios that depict symptoms of three mental health problems (viz. depression, anxiety and HIV-related brain impairment) form the basis of in-depth discussions in 12 existing groups of secondary school students, orphans and vulnerable children, teenage mothers, and out-of-school youths, in both rural and urban settings. The responses show that these young people recognize the mental health sequelae of HIV/AIDS as impacting upon many aspects of their lives.

# Part V

## Early Childhood Care and Development

## 101. Amouzou, Agbessi and Kenneth Hill

2004, 'Child Mortality and Socioeconomic Status in Sub-Saharan Africa', *Population Studies*, Vol. 19, no. 1, pp. 1-11.

This paper examines under-five mortality trends in sub-Saharan Africa, and the association between socioeconomic status - indicated by per capita income, illiteracy, urbanization- and under-five mortality between 1960 and 2000. It shows substantial decline in under-five mortality in all sub-Saharan Africa regions between 1970 and 1990. Regional differentials among West, Central and East Africa that existed in the 1960s had largely disappeared by 1990. However, the decline in under-five mortality appears to have stalled in the 1990s and some countries have experienced increases. The analyses show a consistent negative relationship between under-five mortality and per capita income, but a given income implies lower under-five mortality as one moves towards the present.

## 102. Argeseanu, Solveig

2004, 'Risks, Amenities, and Child Mortality in Rural South Africa', *African Population Studies*, Vol. 19, no. 1, pp. 13-33.

Using a dataset from rural South Africa, this paper examines the effects of many established factors associated with child mortality at different ages and introduces some less explored issues, such as cause of death. The study population comprises part of a district of KwaZulu-Natal. The paper considers 7,045 households in which children were born of 9,974 mothers between February 1995 and March 2002. The dataset captures many vulnerable people who are usually excluded, such as children whose mothers have died or who are often away from home. The study reveals that the most significant predictors of child mortality are characteristics of the mother, especially her birth history, marital status and education.

## 103. Awumbila, Mariama

2003, 'Social Dynamics and Infant Feeding Practices in Northern Ghana', *Institute of African Studies Research Review*, Univ. Ghana, Vol. 19, no. 2, pp. 85-98.

Based on research undertaken in 1998-1999 in a rural and an urban area in Ghana's Bawku East District, this paper examines infant feeding practices of women with children between 0 and 6 months of age and analyses the role of sociocultural factors, household and gender dynamics as determinants of infant feeding practices and child nutrition. The author argues that the existence of beliefs and value systems especially with regard to the cultural administration of water is central to conflicts with exclusive breastfeeding recommendations of WHO and UNICEF.

## 104. Bawah, Ayaga A. and Tukufu Zuberi

2004, 'Socioeconomic Status and Child Mortality: an Illustration Using Housing and Household Characteristics from African Census Data', *African Population Studies*, Vol. 19, suppl. B, pp. 9-29.

This study uses sources of water, type of toilet facilities; housing construction materials; the possession of radio, and animals, as important variables for economic status to create a composite poverty index, and uses this index in a multivariate model to examine its association with childhood mortality in Botswana, Lesotho and Zambia. It shows that the chances of childhood mortality decrease consistently with high levels of the socioeconomic status index.

## 105. Bhana, Deevia

2008, 'Discourses of Childhood Innocence in Primary School HIV/AIDS Education in South Africa', *African Journal of AIDS Research*, Vol. 7, no. 1, pp. 149-158.

This article draws from interview data to examine the meanings that primary school teachers in two race and class-specific contexts in greater Durban, South Africa, may give to children's right to sexual health information as a part of HIV/AIDS education. The article focuses on the regulation and production of childhood innocence by means of the ways the primary school teachers talked about sex in their HIV/AIDS education lessons to grade-four students. The author argues that discourses of childhood innocence regulate and limit the possibilities of conversing about sex in such a context.

## 106. Burke, Kathleen and Kathleen Beegle

2004, 'Why Children aren't Attending School: the Case of Northwestern Tanzania', *Journal of African Economy*, Vol. 13, no. 2, pp. 333-355.

Drawing on longitudinal data of primary-school-age children in Tanzania - the 1991-1994 Kagera Health and Development Survey (KHDS), the present analysis evaluates the role of various dimensions in determining childrens school attendance. The results indicate that policies directed towards increasing a child's attendance need to be focused on the demand for schooling within the context of the household. Policies that affect demand for child labour within the household, especially those that promote substitutes for child labour, should be considered.

## 107. Chimanikire, Donald P., (ed.)

2009, *Youth and Higher Education in Africa: the Cases of Cameroon, South Africa, Eritrea and Zimbabwe*, Dakar: Council for the Development of Social Science Research in Africa (CODESRIA).

This book contains articles recounting the responses of African students to the impact of changing socioeconomic and political conditions in Africa on students and student political organizations in African universities. Contributors recount the responses of students to these changes in their attempt to negotiate better living and studying conditions. The four case studies contained in the book - Cameroon, South Africa, Zimbabwe and Eritrea - clearly reveal the very important aspects of the situation in which African students find themselves in many countries, and underscores the need to understand the character and development of higher education on the continent.

## 108.  Chindime, Clara C. and Susie Ubomba-Jaswa

2007, 'Household Headship and Nutritional Status of Toddlers: an Examination of Malawian Data', *African Population Studies*, Vol. 21, no. 2, pp. 45-73.

This paper examines whether the nutritional status of children in female-headed households (FHH) differs significantly from that of children in male-headed households. Anthropometric data on 1466 toddlers aged 12-59 months and several societal, household and individual variables from the Malawi Demographic Health Survey (MDHS) 1992 were used to find out the net impact of the sex of household head on stunting, undernutrition and wasting in the toddlers. The bivariate results show that children in FHH may not have poorer nutritional outcomes than their counterparts from MHH since the differences are not significant. However, a number of the background characteristics were significantly associated with the three indicators suggesting that the results on headship could be masked by the differentials shown in background characteristics. Besides economic status, the role of birth weight, child's age, sanitation and the region in which the child lives were found to be important differentials in the nutritional status of toddlers in Malawi.

## 109.  Doctor, Henry V.

2004, 'The Effect of Living Standards on Childhood Mortality in Malawi', *African Population Studies*, Vol. 19, suppl. A, pp. 241-263.

This paper uses principal components analysis to create a living standards index (LSI) based on household characteristics and to examine its relationship with childhood mortality in Malawi using 1987 and 1998 census data. When the LSI is applied to the 1987 census data, the results show an increase in mortality for children who come from poor households. However, the results in1998 differ from those in 1987 in that child mortality is higher among rich households and also among households with middle-aged women. These results are consistent with parallel analysis of the 1992 and 2000 Malawi Demographic and Health Survey data. The author argues that, based on the magnitude of the HIV/AIDS prevalence in Malawi in the 1990s, and given the stage of the AIDS epidemic at the time of the 1998 census, the high mortality is closely linked to the epidemic.

## 110. Doctor, Henry V. and Sandile E. Simelane

2005, 'The Impact of Living Standards on Childhood Mortality in South Africa: Evidence from Cross-Sectional Data', *Journal of Social Development in Africa*, Vol. 20, no. 2, pp. 7-38.

Using data on household characteristics collected in the 1997 and 1998 October Household Surveys (OHS) in South Africa and in the 1998 South Africa Demographic and Health Survey (SADHS), the authors examine the relationship between living standards and child mortality. Specifically, they examine whether childhood mortality is higher in poor households than in rich households, and whether between 1997 and 1998 the risk of childhood mortality changed. Results are inconsistent between 1997 and 1998. In 1997 the risk of childhood mortality decreased with increasing socioeconomic status, while in 1998 higher levels of socioeconomic status were associated with higher childhood mortality.

## 111. Essah, Doris

2002, 'Family Life Education Needs of School Children: A Study in Akwapim Akropong', *Institute for African Studies Research Review*, Univ. Ghana, Vol. 18, no. 1, pp. 43-50.

A study of junior secondary school children at Akwapim Akropong, Ghana, indicates that financial reasons, together with curiosity and naughtiness, lead to early adolescent sexual experience, and pregnancy. Potential sources of information on sexual and reproductive health include peers and friends, social clubs and the Planned Parenthood Association of Ghana, television and radio programmes, and school. Menstruation proved to be a taboo topic that both books and adults shied away from discussing with adolescents. Pupils' knowledge of sexually transmitted diseases was variable. They had little knowledge of contraceptive methods, except the condom.

## 112. Falola, Toyin and Matthew M. Heaton, (eds)

2006, *Endangered Bodies: Women, Children and Health in Africa*, Trenton, NJ: Africa World Press.

Originally presented at a conference on African health and illness held at the University of Texas at Austin from March 25-27, 2005, the essays in this collective volume focus on child and maternal health and in particular, the combination of real medical risks with the social environment that often exacerbates them, which women and children face. The essays all revolve around the central issues of raising awareness about the often unspoken health needs of these marginalized groups, as well as what needs to be done to ameliorate their situation both legally and socially. They address these issues in a number of ways, through discussions of women's reproductive rights, the rights of HIV-infected children and AIDS orphans, the prevalence of (sexual) violence against women with its associated health risks, government policy on maternal and child welfare, and the ways that women are restructuring their social milieu to take greater control over both voicing and providing for the health needs of their communities.

## 113. Fataar, Aslam

2009, 'Schooling Subjectivities Across the Post-Apartheid', *Africa Education Review*, Vol. 6, no. 1, pp. 1-18.

The focus of this article is on the subjectivities associated with the changing schooling landscape in the post-apartheid city, South Africa. Urban practices in the city of Cape Town form the backdrop. The author's premise is the view that what people become, their sense of self, can be understood by considering their daily interaction with the city's schools. The article draws on the author's ongoing National Research Foundation (NRF) project entitled 'Educational renovation in urban spaces', based on qualitative work in a number of school sites in Cape Town.

## 114. Gokah, Thephilus Kofi

2008, 'Ghana's School Feeding Programme (GSFP) and the Well-Being of Children: a Critical Appraisal', *Journal of Social Development in Africa*, Vol. 23, no. 1, pp. 161-190.

This paper appraises Ghana's school feeding programme and the initial report on the review of the programme. The programme began in September 2005 and aims to reduce hunger and malnutrition; increase school enrolment, attendance and retention; and boost domestic food production. The paper argues that the assumptions on which the programme was formulated were unrealistic and resulted in both theoretical and operational difficulties with implications for the programme's sustainability. It further argues that the design of the school feeding programme was not sufficiently flexible to enable the government to cope with emergency situations such as floods and drought. The paper concludes that the programme does benefit children in terms of increased school enrolment and may have helped to keep some children in school, but the programme has not positively impacted on the root causes of malnutrition and hunger among Ghana's school children.

## 115. Graham, Paul, (ed.)

2006, *Inheriting Poverty?: The Link Between Children's Wellbeing and Unemployment in South Africa*, Cape Town: Idasa Publishing.

The papers in this volume focus on the interface between unemployment, poverty and children's well-being in South Africa. They were first presented at a seminar hosted by the Institute for Democracy in South Africa (IDASA), the Children's Institute of the University of Cape Town, and Save the Children Sweden in October 2005. The authors highlight such factors as poverty, unemployment, violence and abuse, inadequate policy support and services, and especially HIV/AIDS as a real threat to the realization of the rights of the African child.

## 116. Gubert, Flore and Anne-Sophie Robilliard

2008, 'Risk and Schooling Decisions in Rural Madagascar: a Panel Data-Analysis', *Journal of African Economies*, Vol. 17, no. 2, pp. 207-238.

In this paper, the authors examine the possibility that parents obtain informal income insurance by letting their children work. They test this hypothesis by examining the relationship between household income shocks and human capital investment in children. In particular, they investigate whether children's propensity to join school and to drop out of school responds to transient shocks.

## 117. Hoadley, Ursula

2007, 'Boundaries of Care: the Role of the School in Supporting Vulnerable Children in the Context of HIV and AIDS', *African Journal of AIDS Research*, Vol. 6, no. 3, pp. 251-259.

This paper interrogates this notion and raises some key issues in considering the role of schools in the context of the epidemic based on two research activities. The first was a desk review of projects working in the area of schools in the context of HIV/AIDS and poverty, including a review of the policies underlying these initiatives. The second was the documentation of a particular project in a province of South Africa. The paper offers possible ways forward in considering the role of schools in the context of HIV and AIDS. These include new ways of thinking about resourcing, proper monitoring and evaluation of projects, and a focus on quality teaching and learning.

## 118. Kabubo-Mariara, Jane, Godfrey K. Ndenge and Domisiano K. Mwabu

2009, 'Determinants of Children's Nutritional Status in Kenya: Evidence from Demographic and Health Surveys', *Journal of African Economies*, Vol. 18, no. 3, pp. 363-387.

The authors use a pooled sample of the 1998 and 2003 Demographic and Health Survey data sets for Kenya to analyse the determinants of children's nutritional status. By employing descriptive and econometric analysis, augmented by policy simulations, they investigate the impact of child, parental, household and community characteristics on children's height and on the probability of stunting. In estimation, the authors control for sample design and possible heterogeneity arising from unobserved community characteristics correlated with children's nutritional status and its determinants. The key findings are that boys suffer more malnutrition than girls; children of multiple births are more likely to be malnourished than singletons; maternal education is a more important determinant of children's nutritional status than paternal education; household assets are also important determinants of children's nutritional status, as well as the use of public health services, and usage of modern contraceptives.

## 119. Kong'ong'o, Maurice

2006, 'The Burden of Childhood Malaria: an Anthropological Insight into a Major Medical Problem', *Research Review: Institute of African Studies*. Vol. 22, no. 1, p. 15-22.

Based on a review of published research, this paper presents the sociocultural factors at play in the management of childhood malaria. A number of studies have been conducted in various countries in sub-Saharan Africa on the role of sociocultural parameters in the understanding and interpretation of illness. These include local knowledge of the aetiology, transmission and interpretation of illness. It appears that causation and transmission of malaria are not always distinguished and are used interchangeably. Furthermore, the incidence of malaria is often not linked to mosquitoes, but to, for instance, drinking contaminated water or witchcraft. Treatment-seeking behaviour is influenced by a variety of factors, including beliefs, access to health care, costs of care and attitudes towards health care providers. The health care system can be divided into three overlapping parts: the popular, the professional and the folk sectors. In careseeking for childhood malaria this overlap is obvious and the consequences are manifest.

## 120. Kovsted, Jens, Claus C. Portner and Finn Tarp

2002, 'Child Health and Mortality: Does Health Knowledge Matter?' *Journal of African Economies*, Vol. 11, no. 4, pp. 542-560.

This paper studies factors that influence child health in Bissau, the capital of Guinea-Bissau. This environment is characterized by high infant mortality, but not by malnutrition. The authors show that although maternal education is important in determining child health and mortality this effect diminishes or disappears when health knowledge is introduced as an explanatory variable. It emerges that health knowledge has large and positive effects on both child mortality and health when the endogeneity of health knowledge is recognized and taken into account.

### 121. Magadi, Monica

2004, 'Maternal and Child Health Among the Urban Poor in Nairobi, Kenya', *African Population Studies*, Vol. 19, suppl. B, pp. 179-198.

This paper examines maternal and child health in the Nairobi slums in Kenya using information on 1219 births which occurred in the period 1997-2000. The specific objectives are to compare maternal and child health indicators in the Nairobi slums with the rest of the Kenyan population, and to identify socioeconomic and demographic factors associated with poor maternal and child health. The results show that overall, the quality of antenatal care in the slums is comparable to that in the rest of Kenya. With respect to professional delivery care, the Nairobi slums are worse off than the rest of Nairobi or other urban areas in Kenya, but they seem better off compared to rural communities.

### 122. Molosi, Keneilwe

2008, 'Botswana's San Communities and the Challenge of Accessing Basic Education: the Need for a Paradigm Shift', *Journal of Social Development in Africa*, Vol. 23, no. 2, pp. 83-106.

This paper argues that these high drop-out rates should be blamed on the unresponsive nature of the country's education curriculum. San schoolchildren face several challenges, including a lack of educational resources, the absence of mother-tongue instruction, a school culture that is different from the unique way of life of the San, and the 'critical mass' effect (the fact that they are fewer in number than other groups), so they tend to view education as a remote and artificial enterprise that frustrates their efforts. The paper advocates a two way schooling model to accommodate the San in the formal education system in Botswana.

### 123. Moses, Susan

2006, 'The Impact of Neighbourhood-Level Factors on Children's Everyday Lives, Well-Being and Identity: a Qualitative Study of Children Living in Ocean View, Cape Town', *Social Dynamics*, Vol. 32, no. 1, pp. 102-134.

Drawing on qualitative data generated over fifteen months by children aged six to eighteen, this article explores the ways in which neighbourhood and community spaces of Ocean View impact on the lives of children living there. The article draws particular attention to the way in which the legacy of Ocean View's particular sociopolitical history continues to impact on children, through the interaction of physical, social and economic features which limit their everyday lives to the spaces and people within Ocean View. This affects children's access to resources, hampers integration, and impacts on their self and collective efficacy. Children's individual preferences, skills and personalities are shown to affect how they cope with difficulties and respond to available opportunities and supports. The author argues for moving away from focusing on the impact of discrete neighbourhood features to a focus on the environmental processes that benefit children.

## 124. Munthali, Alister C.

2001, 'Management of Childhood Illnesses Among the Tumbuka of Rumphi District in Northern Malawi', *Society of Malawi Journal*, Vol. 54, no. 2, pp. 43-65.

This study, based on interviews held in 2000 in Rumphi District (northern Malawi) among the Tumbuka of Traditional Authority Chikulamayembe, examines what the people in the rural areas of Malawi consider to be the most dangerous diseases for their children and how they try to treat and prevent these diseases. It pays attention to illnesses associated with malaria; malnutrition; diarrhoea and coughs (believed to be caused by parents' sexual intercourse); measles; and conjunctivitis. The results of the study show that although belief in the supernatural causation of disease still abounds, the Tumbuka in general are engaged in empirical truths only they cannot explain these in biological terms.

## 125. Mutekanga, Esau N. and Peter R. Atekyereza

2007, 'The Relationship Between Child Breastfeeding and Infant Health: The Case of Rukungiri District in Uganda', *Journal of Social Development in Africa*, Vol. 22, no. 2, pp. 63-82.

This paper is based on a study that was conducted in 2004 in Rukungiri district, Uganda, to investigate the relationship between early childhood nutritional practices, particularly breastfeeding, and child health. It looks at factors such as breastfeeding duration (in terms of months), breastfeeding frequency (in terms of number of times per day), time taken by mothers for each breastfeeding 'session', personal hygiene, and the relationship between breastfeeding habits and mothers' level of education as well as their occupation. The study shows that child malnutrition in Uganda is high and is partly explained by breastfeeding habits.

## 126. Ndirangu, M., J.K. Mwangi and J. Changeiywo

2007, 'Educational Provision for the Academically Gifted: Rhetoric or Reality?: Case of Primary Schools in Nyandarua District, Kenya', *Eastern Africa Social Science Research Review*, Vol. 23, no. 2, pp. 55-69.

Using interviews and questionnaires for head teachers, this study examines whether primary schools in Nyandarua District, Kenya, make any special educational provision in order to help gifted children learn, and identifies the challenges such children pose and face in primary education. It looks into the existence of educational programmes (special curricular materials geared to helping gifted children) for the academically gifted children in Kenyan primary schools; determines the teachers' views concerning educational provision for academically gifted children; and identifies any locally available resources (learning resources within the locality of the school) that could be utilized in educational provision for the academically gifted children in Kenyan primary schools.

## 127. Ngianga-Bakwin, Kandala and Nyovani Madise

2004, 'The Spatial Epidemiology of Childhood Diseases in Malawi and Zambia', *African Population Studies*, Vol. 19, suppl. B, pp. 199-226.

This paper describes spatial variation, at the district level, in the prevalence of diarrhoea, fever and cough among children under 5 years of age, using the 1992 Demographic and Health surveys from Malawi and Zambia. These ailments are still a major cause of mortality among children in sub-Saharan Africa. The evidence suggests that relatively high or low childhood districts spatially cluster together within both countries, suggesting that research efforts may be focused on the clusters to assess local causes (environmental, cultural etc.) of high or low childhood morbidity. Thus, maps could be used for targeting development efforts at a glance, or for exploring relationships between welfare indicators and variables.

## 128.  Nicholson, Caroline M.A.

2002, 'The Right to Health Care, the Best Interests of the Child, and AIDS in South Africa and Malawi', *The Comparative and International Law Journal of Southern Africa*, Vol. 35, no. 3, pp. 351-376.

This paper focuses on children's access and right to health care in the context of attention to HIV/AIDS. The author argues that despite horrifying AIDS statistics, the risk of a child dying of malnutrition in Africa is higher than the risk of him or her dying of AIDS. If this reality is to change poverty must be eliminated as a disease vector. South Africa and Malawi lack the resources to deal with poverty alone. They need massive injections of foreign aid. Wealthy nations cannot risk the potential negative economic impact that might result if AIDS in Africa is allowed to precipitate a development crisis.

## 129.  Nyanchoka Keraka, Margaret and Wellington Nguya Wamicha

2003, 'Child Morbidity and Mortality in Slum Environments Along Nairobi River', *Eastern Africa Social Science Research Review*, Vol. 19, no. 1, pp. 41-57.

This article publishes the results of a study, which examined the impact of slum environments on morbidity and mortality profiles in slum environments along Nairobi River (Kenya). The main objectives were: first, to assess the influence of environmental factors on child morbidity and mortality, and second, to analyse the influence of the perception and behaviour patterns of slum dwellers on child mortality and morbidity. The data used in this study was collected using in-depth interviews and extensive literature review. The key finding of the study was that poverty is a major factor in child morbidity and mortality.

### 130. Ogoye-Ndegwa, Charles, Dominic Abudho, and Jens Aagaard-Hansen

2002, "New Learning in Old Organisations': Children's Participation in a School-Based Nutrition Project in Western Kenya', *Development in Practice*, Vol. 12, no. 3/4, pp. 449-460.

This paper reports on a research project that the authors designed and implemented in Western Kenya on traditional vegetables as a means of supplementary nutrition and by recruiting pupils as co-researchers. The study was conducted in Bondo District, Nyanza Province, in a Luo community along the shores of Lake Victoria, in May 1999 and March 2000 and sought to answer the question 'Who are the most effective change agents, how they can be supported, and how their efforts can be diffused in the community and scaled up are key questions in the community development literature'. The research explored the feasibility of increasing the intake of traditional vegetables through a school-based horticulture programme and pupils' competence as effective change agents when empowered in culturally compatible ways. The results offer lessons for practitioners regarding creative to identify and empower change agents within traditional organizations and encourage innovative creation and diffusion of knowledge.

### 131. Ouma, Jerusha Akoth

2006, 'Socio-Cultural Factors that Influence Child Survival in Nyang'oma Sublocation, Bondo District', *Mila*, Vol. 7, pp. 41-48.

This paper examines sociocultural factors affecting child survival in Nyang'oma sublocation, Bondo district, Kenya. Specifically, the paper investigates how mothers' perceptions of common childhood diseases (malaria, measles and diarrhoea) and diseases associated with 'chira' (diseases related mostly to the transgression of principles governing sexuality and/or seniority) and the evil eye influence child survival in the district. The paper is based on data from group discussions, interviews, surveys, narratives and observation. It shows that practices associated with the cultural concept of 'chira' lower children's chances of survival through delayed treatment.

## 132. Shumba, J., C. Maphosa, and A. Shumba

2008, 'Curriculum Decision-Making Decentralization Policy in Zimbabwe: how Involved are the Students in Deciding Curriculum Content?' *Africa Education Review*, Vol. 5, no. 1, pp. 48-67.

The study examines the current Zimbabwean school system in order to establish the extent to which it is conducive to students making decisions about the selection of subjects they learn at school and to examine the nature of children's rights and the extent to which these rights are practised in schools and in the prevailing socioeconomic and political milieu. The study found that teachers and pupils seemed to be aware of pupils' rights to participate in deciding the subjects they studied. However in practice the majority of the students indicated they had no say in choice of subjects, a fact that was corroborated by most of the teachers and all of the school heads.

## 133. Teglhus, Lene

2006, 'Our Cannot Survive on Breast Milk Alone', *Mila*, Vol. 7, pp. 32-40.

Based on three months of research among Luo mothers in a community in Nyang'oma in western Kenya, this paper aims at understanding the complex and varied stakes involved in women's decisions on child care actions, breastfeeding in particular. It appears that mothers do listen to advice given them by health care workers to exclusively breastfeed infants for the first six months and drink a lot of cow's milk themselves, but practise differently, because they think that breastfeeding alone does not satisfy their children. The paper shows that Luo mothers orientate more towards the local understanding than towards the information given them in a hospital far away because they need to be part of their community and want to be recognized as a good mother.

## 134. Wilbraham, Lindy

2008, 'Parental Communication with Children about Sex in the South African HIV Epidemic: Raced, Classed and Cultural Appropriations of Lovelines', *African Journal of AIDS Research*, Vol. 7, no. 1, pp. 95-109.

This paper uses a reading of interactive discourse from (racially and gender) mixed groups of parents who, as professionals and postgraduate students in a university context, discussed their own childrearing practices in response to a particular didactic media text about sex-communication. In a way different from traditional media-reception studies, this discourse analytic reading of parents' engagement with risk-expertise examines how mothers especially are persuaded (or not) to adopt particular childrearing practices in the context of an HIV epidemic. The analysis explores the partial buy-in to expert Western psychological techniques concerning talking with children about sex openly and often, and how this appropriation is negotiated in contextual family situations that are gendered, raced, classed and acculturated.

### 135. Woldemicael, Gebremariam

2003, 'War Crisis and Child Mortality in Eritrea: 1981-1995', *Journal of Eritrean studies*, Vol. 2, no. 1/2, pp. 1-8.

This paper assesses the impact of the Eritrean war for independence between 1981 and 1990 and that of peace and political stability after the war (1991-1995) on early childhood mortality by using the 1995 Eritrea Demographic and Health Survey (EDHS). It focuses on children born between one month and fifteen years before the survey. The results show that while infant and childhood mortality was almost constant during the war period, there was a substantial decline during the postwar period, which was more marked in rural than in urban areas.

### 136. Van Camp, John

2008, 'Improving the Quality of Complementary Food for Young Children in Africa', *Bulletin des séances: Académie royale des sciences d'outre-mer*, Vol. 54, no. 2, pp. 159-168.

This paper reports on a baseline and intervention study with 6-12 month-old children in Tanzania in which a processed Complementary Food (CF) composed of finger millet, kidney beans, peanuts and mango puree, was evaluated relative to a control product containing the same ingredients, but without processing. Although the processed product had a threefold increase in energy density and an improved iron solubility compared to the control product, no significant difference either in weight gain, longitudinal growth, or iron status was noticed between the two groups at the end of the trial. Further optimization of local processing is needed, and more appropriate biomarkers to evaluate iron bioavailability have to be used.

# Part VI

## Fertility, Sexuality, and Reproductive Health

## 137. Awedoba, A.K.

2002, 'Kasena Norms and Reproductive Health', *Institute of African Studies Research Review*, Univ. Ghana, Vol. 18, no. 1, pp. 13-26.

This paper is a description of existing norms surrounding reproduction among the Kasena in Ghana. Cultural norms with respect to conjugal practices and attitudes to extramarital sex, lineage exogamy, premarital chastity and sexual abstinence impact directly on reproductive health, as do dietary prohibitions, which apply to the expectant and nursing mother. Despite the high value placed on children, not all children are considered equally desirable. The Kasena consider certain births as unusual, if not unnatural. For example, spirits masquerading as babies with congenital deformities are perceived as threats to the family and society and 'must be returned to the bush'.

## 138. Dahlbäc, Elisabeth

2006, 'Zambian Male Adolescents' Perceptions about Premarital Sexual Relationships', *African Journal of AIDS Research*, Vol. 5, no. 3, pp. 257-264.

This study explores male adolescents' perceptions and expectations about premarital sexual relationships in Zambia. Seven focus group discussions were conducted between November 2000 and May 2001, in George (near Lusaka) and Chimwemwe (Copperbelt Province) compounds, with 53 boys aged 15 to 19. The findings reveal that adolescent premarital sexual relationships are common and considered by many boys as a prerequisite to achieving an adult male's autonomy and status. The boys viewed themselves as the privileged gender, with greater freedom than girls, and were the major decision makers on sexual matters in relationships. The results indicate that traditional values and stereotypical gender roles continue to influence Zambian boys' male identity.

## 139. Darkwah, Akosua K. and Alexina Arthur

2006, '(A)sexualizing Ghanaian Youth?: a Case Study of Virgin Clubs in Accra and Kumasi', *Ghana Studies*, Vol. 9, pp. 123-149.

In this study of three so-called Virgin Clubs in Accra and Kumasi (Ghana), where the authors held interviews in 2004, they show that although these Clubs were ostensibly set up to help in the fight against HIV/AIDS, they also provide an opportunity for the strengthening of patriarchal control over female sexuality, specifically females from lower socioeconomic backgrounds. The main strategy of the Clubs to reduce the prevalence of HIV/AIDS in Ghana was through advocating abstinence, a message sitting well with the wealth of Pentecostal churches in Ghana as well as with many African communities. The authors also show, however, that, even as members of Virgin Clubs, young Ghanaian women have not been asexualized, but respond to their sexual desires in a variety of ways.

## 140. Djamba, Yanyi K. (ed.)

2005, *Sexual Behavior of Adolescents in Contemporary Sub-Saharan Africa*, Lewiston, NY: Edwin Mellen Press.

This volume provides a state-of-the-art picture of adolescent sexual behaviours in sub-Saharan Africa. It is divided into three parts: Part One: Determinants of risky sexual behavior. Part Two: HIV, contraception, modernization, and sex. Part Three: Kinship, nationality, and sexuality. Contributions include such areas as sexual risk behaviors and their consequences; HIV prevalence and socio-cultural contexts of sexuality; and ethnicity and sexual behavior.

## 141. Glaser, Clive

2005, 'Managing the Sexuality of Urban Youth: Johannesburg, 1920s-1960s', *The International Journal of African Historical Studies*, Vol. 38, no. 2, pp. 301-327.

Based on scholarship of several researchers, supplemented with his own previously published work as well as additional primary research, the author analyses the relationship between State and private as well as church welfare organizations in dealing with the perceived problem of uncontrolled sexuality during the period. He argues that the high levels of interaction and cooperation within the welfare network of the 1920s-1940s later gave way to growing suspicion and alienation. Aside from grants to family planning associations, the central government had by the 1960s almost completely severed contact with organizations that had so powerfully influenced welfare policy in the interwar years.

## 142. Hevi-Yiboe, Laetitia A.P.

2003, 'Family Resources and Reproductive Health of Girls: a Focus on Money and 'TugbewTwT': Puberty Rites Among the Dodome Ewes', *Institute of African Studies Research Review*, Univ. Ghana, Vol. 19, no. 1, pp. 79-90.

The major objective of this paper is to throw some light on how proper use of family resources (such as money, time, energy) and community resources (such as schools) could help resolve the problem. The author examines the process of 'tugbewTwT' as well as its objectives, advantages and disadvantages. An exploratory study in Dodome revealed that the majority of the people would like 'tugbewTwT' to be reintroduced. The paper recommends that families be empowered financially to meet members' needs and that a detailed study be carried out into 'tugbewTwT' with the aim of understanding and modernizing the rites for reintroduction in Dodome and the Ho district as a whole.

## 143. HSRC

2003, *Fertility: Current South African Issues of Poverty, HIV/AIDS & Youth: Seminar Proceedings: Human Sciences Research Council, Child, Youth and Family Development Research Programme in collaboration with Department of Social Development*, Cape Town: HSRC Publishers.

This collective volume contains three papers presented at the seminar and attempts to synthesize elements of the discussion invoked by the papers. Contributions: Introduction, by Christine A. Varga; Fertility transition in South Africa and its impact on the four major population groups, by Leon Swartz; Fertility, poverty and gender in South Africa, by Barbara A. Anderson (with a response by Monde B. Makiwane); Adolescent fertility: a population concern, by Kim Eva Dickson (with a response by Eric O. Udjo); HIV and fertility in South Africa: some theoretical and methodological considerations, by Gretchen du Plessis; The fertility transition in sub-Saharan Africa, by John C. Caldwell and Pat Caldwell.

## 144. Ibisomi, Latifat D.G. and Clifford O. Odimegwu

2007, 'Predictors of Unintended Pregnancy Among South African Youth', *Eastern Africa Social Science Research Review*, Vol. 23, no. 1, pp. 61-80.

Using the 1998 South African Demographic and Health Survey (SADHS) data set, this study examined the distribution of and factors associated with unintended pregnancy among South African youth. Analysis was based on a sub-sample of 1,395 women aged 15-24 who were interviewed during the survey and who were pregnant at the time of and/or three years preceding the survey. The results show a high level of unintended pregnancy with only 29 percent of the pregnancies wanted.

## 145. Isiugo-Abanihe, Ifeoma M. and Uche C. Isiugo-Abanihe

2007, 'Adolescent Sexuality and Reproductive Health in Two Oil Producing Communities in Imo and Rivers States, Nigeria', *African Population Studies*, Vol. 22, no. 2, pp. 47-76.

The study was conducted in two contiguous oil-producing rural local government areas in Imo State and Rivers State of Nigeria, to examine adolescent sexuality and reproductive health in the area given its peculiarities. This is a baseline study for an intervention project aimed at identifying strategies for achieving behavioural changes among the youth, and for promotion of health-seeking behaviour for the control of HIV/ AIDS and other sexually transmitted infections (STIs). Data were collected through questionnaires administered among 725 students in secondary schools and 249 school drop-outs, comprising 483 females and 491 males. The questionnaire generated ample information on knowledge, attitudes and practices of the youth with respect to sexuality and reproductive health as well as various background characteristics of the respondents. Supplementary qualitative data were collected through focus group discussions. The study found a high level of sexual activity among both in-school and out-of-school adolescents, low levels of knowledge of preventive measures, negotiation skills and STIs, and relatively high levels of premarital pregnancy, abortion and incidence of STIs.

## 146.  Isiugo-Abanihe, Uche C. and Kola' A. Oyediran

2004, 'Household Socioeconomic Status and Sexual Behaviour Among Nigerian Female Youth', *African Population Studies*, Vol. 19, no. 1, pp. 81-98.

This paper examines the determinants of sexual behaviour with special reference to the effect of household socioeconomic status as a proxy for poverty. The data are derived from the 1999 Nigeria Demographic and Health Survey; the analysis is restricted to 1,831 never married females age 15-24. Both descriptive and analytical methods are used to assess the effects of each poverty-related factor when the effects of other demographic and socio-cultural factors are controlled statistically. The results show that 31.5 percent of the respondents have had sexual intercourse, and more than half of these had an affair in the month preceding the survey. The median age of sexual debut is 17 years, and there is little variation among socio-demographic and poverty-related indices, indicating a generally early initiation of sexual activity. Condom use is low among the youth; only 15 percent have ever used condoms, and about 22 percent of the sexually experienced used condoms the last time they had an affair. The results indicate that those who have access to the media and those of high socioeconomic status are more sexually exposed than their counterparts who do not have access to media or have less household facilities.

## 147.  LaFont, Suzanne and Dianne Hubbard, (eds)

2007, *Unravelling Taboos: Gender and Sexuality in Namibia*, Windhoek: Legal Assistance Centre.

The essays in this volume unravel the misconceptions, stereotypes and taboos surrounding the concepts of gender equality, sexuality and sexual rights in Namibia. The chapters are grouped into seven parts covering such topics as History; Legal issues; Youth, gender and sexuality; Reproduction and marriage; HIV/AIDS: gender and survival; Same-sex sexuality; and, Gender, sexuality and power.

## 148. Mba, Chuks J. and Emmanuel Ngwe, (eds)

2006, *Reproductive, Maternal and Child Health in Africa: Current Developments and Future Direction*, Dakar: UEPA/UAPS.

This volume is the result of a workshop on reproductive health in Africa held in Dakar, Senegal, on 15-16 May 2006. The workshop discussed levels and trends in maternal and infant mortality, integrated approaches to reproductive health, HIV/AIDS, women's empowerment and rights, safe motherhood, adolescent sexuality, and male involvement in reproductive health issues.

## 149. Mberu, Blessing Uchenna

2008, 'Protection Before the Harm: the Case of Condom Use at the Onset of Premarital Sexual Relationship Among Youths in Nigeria', *African Population Studies*, Vol. 23, no. 1, pp. 57-83.

This article builds on the proposition that condom use at first intercourse is an immediate indicator of the risks associated with the encounter and the propensity of subsequent regular condom use. Data from the 2003 Nigeria Demographic and Health Survey and binary logistic regression models were utilized to examine the predictors of condom use at premarital sexual debut among Nigerian youths aged 15-24. The analysis identified significant independent effects of age at sexual debut, living arrangements, level of education, and household economic status, with the strongest effect linked to ethnic origin. The findings underscore the complexity of sociocultural contexts that influence sexual behaviour across groups within one country, and the importance of a multifactor policy perspective for effective behaviour interventions.

## 150. Molla, Mitike

2009, 'Readiness of Youth in Rural Ethiopia to Seek Health Services for Sexually Transmitted Infections', *African Journal of AIDS Research*, Vol. 8, no. 2, pp. 135-146.

This study provides information on knowledge about common STIs, and the perceptions, preferences and use of health services for STIs, among youths and health care providers in predominately rural Butajira, a town in south-central Ethiopia. The authors performed a cross-sectional survey among 3,743 randomly selected youths aged 15-24 years, in 2004, and in-depth interviews with ten health care providers, in 2006. Less than 38 percent of the youths knew the common STIs. The results suggest that young people are vulnerable to HIV exposure due to lack of knowledge about STIs and especially as a result of having an untreated STI. Health services that are uncoordinated and unable to handle youths' sexual and reproductive health problems, as well as judgemental health professionals and prevailing sexual taboos, are also reported as impediments to youths seeking health care.

## 151. Njau, Bernard

2007, 'The Influence of Peers and Other Significant Persons on Sexuality and Condom-Use Among Young Adults in Northern Tanzania' *African Journal of AIDS Research*, Vol. 6, no. 1, pp. 33-40.

This paper reports on a study conducted in northern Tanzania in June and July 2004. 526 respondents aged 15-24 years were selected from in-school and out-of-school groups. Of the total, 41.5 percent were sexually active. The paper provides information on self-efficacy in sexual relationships; self-efficacy in the intention to use condoms and the influence of peers and other significant persons on the intention to use condoms. It appears that the age of sexual debut ranged from age 5-20 years for boys, and age 7-24 for girls. The mean age of sexual debut was 16 years old for males and 17 years old for females. As a generalization, the sexually experienced youths in the study population had experienced sex at a relatively early age and often had not used a condom at first sexual intercourse.

## 152. Njau, Bernard

2009, 'Gender Differences in Intention to Remain a Virgin Until Marriage Among School Pupils in Rural Northern Tanzania', *African Journal of AIDS Research*, Vol. 8, no. 2, pp. 157-166.

This study was conducted in ten districts in the Kilimanjaro, Arusha, and Manyara regions of northern Tanzania, in July 2005. Out of 65 villages, four were randomly selected. In total, 953 primary school pupils, aged 10 to 14 years, participated in an interview and questionnaire: about 54 percent were girls and 41 percent were aged 12 to 13. Thirty-four percent of boys and 28.5 percent of girls said they had the intention to remain a virgin until marriage. Among the male respondents, having the intention to remain a virgin until marriage was associated with sharing a bedroom with a brother under age 18 years and with saying that girls have the right to say 'no' to sex; among males, the intention was also negatively associated with saying they had the confidence to refuse sex with someone they had known for less than three months. Among the female respondents, having the intention to remain a virgin until marriage was associated with living with both parents and saying that they had the confidence to refuse sex with someone who has authority or power. The findings highlight that young adolescents may benefit from community-based HIV-prevention programmes that include building lifeskills and increasing one's confidence to abstain from sex or delay sexual debut until marriage.

## 153. Nwakeze, Ngozi M.

2007, 'The Demand for Children in Anambra State of Nigeria: a Logit Analysis', *African Population Studies*, Vol. 22, no. 2, pp. 167-193.

This paper provides empirical evidence on the determinants of demand for children in Anambra State of Nigeria through data obtained from a household survey conducted in 2000 were explored. Logistics regression technique was used for the data analysis and the factors identified as strong predictors of demand for children include wife's level of participation in decision making, occupation, place of residence, husband's education, among others. Surprisingly, wife's education is among the weak predictors.

## 154. Ogunrinade, Adewale O.

2008, 'Social and Biblical Remedies to the Problem of Teenage Pregnancy in Nigeria', *Orita*, Vol. 40, no. 2, pp. 33-49.

This paper outlines some of the known causes and consequences of teenage pregnancy in Nigeria and presents solutions to the problem from two ends: the social and the biblical. Sociological remedies proposed include intensified sex education in schools, homes and the wider society, as well as intensified moral instructions from parents and guardians, and the improvement of government policies on youth empowerment and development. As to biblical remedies, Church leaders behave as if teenage pregnancy is a 'social issue' and the problems associated with it do not exist in the Church.

## 155. Osaaji, Mumia G.

2008, 'Imagi(ni)ng Bodies as Pleasure: Interrogating Sexual Identity Among University Youth', *Mila*, Vol. 9, pp. 16-23.

This article, which is based on research among students of the University of Nairobi in 2007, examines changing sexual identities among male youth in Kenya. It shows that sexual identity among Kenyan youth is in a state of flux; youth are under pressure to 'escape' from more conservative sexual identities to the innovative and attractive sexual images of youth in the Western world, as popularized by hip-hop. The sexual identity of male students is increasingly influenced by the glitz and glamour of rap music, sport, and the Internet. The key markers of this emerging identity are the unique dressing and hair styles, the adoption of special speech acts (American accent and 'Sheng' dialect), a concern for a 'sexy' physical appearance (including tattooing), an obsession with casual sex, and a heightened lust for ostentatious material possessions.

## 156. Petit, Véronique and Lucas Tchetgnia

2009, 'Les Enjeux de la Sexualité Transactionnelle Pré-Maritale en Milieu Urbain Camerounais', *Autrepart*, No. 49, pp. 205-222.

This article is based on anthropological research conducted in urban Cameroon comprising interviews and observations conducted with young women and young men from different cultures in Douala to highlight the dynamic and complex relationship between young people and premarital sex within a context of economic vulnerability, unequal gender relations and a significant prevalence of HIV / AIDS. Transactional sexuality and the monetization of exchange in the relationship between young people is also discussed. The research shows that young people have developed specific ways of justifying their practices in economic terms that could easily be considered prostitution and venality.

## 157. Ringsted, Mette

2004, 'Growing up Pregnant: Events of Kinship in Everyday life', *African Sociological Review*, Vol. 8, no. 1, pp. 100-117.

Based on fieldwork carried out in 2002-2003 in Muheza, a roadside town in northeastern Tanzania, this paper explores how pregnant girls and young mothers, between the ages of 14 and 19, manage their social relations during pregnancy and early motherhood. Whereas most of the pregnant girls and young mothers in this study lived as 'unwanted family members', others were reintegrated into their families. The paper focuses on how they actively negotiate and form 'relatedness' to reduce uncertainty in their daily life, and particularly how they and their children struggle not to be excluded from reciprocal family responsibilities

## 158. Sam, David Lackland

2001, 'Value of Children: Effects of Globalization on Fertility Behavior and Child-Rearing Practices in Ghana', *Research Review: Institute of African Studies*, Univ. of Ghana, Vol. 17, no. 2, pp. 5-16

This paper draws upon ideas emerging from an ongoing research project (Value of children, VOC) in nine non-African countries. The paper aims at raising concerns about the implications of the VOC study findings for Africa, particularly Ghana, and at possibly initiating a similar study in Ghana. First, the paper looks at the question of how 'values of children' may be reflected in child rearing practices. Next, an examination of the role of globalization -defined in this analysis as the process by which cultures influence one another and become more alike through trade, immigration, and the exchange of information and ideas - focuses on the question of how Western industrialized countries in the form of modernization and urbanization are influencing Ghana culturally, socially, economically and politically, and how this in turn affects fertility behaviour and child rearing practices.

## 159. Tadesse, Bedassa and Sisay Asefa

2002, 'Empirical Analysis of the Determinants of Demand for Children in Jimma City, Ethiopia: an Application of Count Data Model'. *Eastern Africa Social Science Research Review*, Vol. 18. no. 2, pp. 43-67.

Using cross-section data on urban households from Jimma city, southwestern Ethiopia, this paper applies the economic theory of consumer choice and examines some endogenous household characteristics that affect the demand for children among urban households in Ethiopia. Based on parameter estimates derived from a count data model, the paper also simulates the average number of children desired by a woman of median urban household characteristics and assesses the extent to which an exogenously set population policy goal of lower fertility can be achieved. The results of the study indicate that enhancing paternal and maternal education, altering the economic value of children, increasing household income, and delaying the marriage age are important policy measures that should be pursued to reduce fertility.

# Part VII

## HIV/AIDS and Orphans

## 160. Adubang'o Awotho, Samy and Amuda Baba

2007, 'Prise en Charge Communautaire des Enfants Orphelins du Vih/sida: Expérience de la Cité d'Aru', *African Population Studies*, Vol. 22, no. 1, pp. 23-37.

This study aims to describe specifically how is the management of these children in the community of the city of Aru (Ituri district) in the northeast of the Democratic Republic of Congo. The study is qualitative and twenty semi-structured interviews with officials of host families for orphaned children, and a focus group session for discussion including 12 children orphaned by HIV/AIDS living alone were performed 1 March 28, 2006. The study recommends the strengthening of community capacity that can enable built-in support and full of orphaned children, which should be approached in a multidimensional way: psychosocial, economic, educational, etc.

## 161. Anarfi, John Kwasi

2003, 'To Change or not to Change: Obstacles and Resistance to Sexual Behavioural Change Among the Youth in Ghana in the Era of AIDS', *Research Review: Institute of African Studies*, Univ. Ghana, Vol. 19, no. 1, pp. 27-45.

This paper presents a review of available literature on sexual behaviour, which shows a number of hindrances to positive behavioural responses to the threat of HIV/AIDS. Some of these factors are related to social institutions and structures, such as marriage, and particularly polygamy; the culture of silence adopted by society concerning the sex education of youths; a breakdown of puberty rites; and economic motivations of young girls and women. Next, the paper presents the results of a study on perceptions of and reactions to the HIV/AIDS epidemic, which was carried out among in and out-of-school youth in five regions in Ghana (Greater Accra, Eastern, Ashanti, Northern and Upper East Regions). The young people interviewed confirmed most of the issues raised in the literature review. Attention is paid to knowledge, attitudes and misconceptions related to HIV/AIDS; protection during sexual intercourse; obstacles to change; societal influence; and the influence of Western education and Christianity.

## 162.  Ansell, Nicola and Lorraine Van Blerk

2004, 'Children's Migration as a Household/Family Strategy: Coping with AIDS in Lesotho and Malawi', *Journal of Southern African Studies*, Vol. 30, no. 3, pp. 673-690.

This article examines the diverse ways in which households/families in Lesotho and Malawi employ children's (accompanied and unaccompanied) migration as a strategy to enable them to cope with the impacts of HIV/AIDS. Based on qualitative research with both guardians and migrant children in four communities - low-middle income areas of Maseru; Tlali, a village in the foothills of Lesotho's Maluti Mountains; a low-income area of Blantyre; and Mpando, a Lomwe-speaking village in southern Malawi-it explores how decisions are made concerning where children should live.

## 163.  Asante, Richard

2006, 'Youth Responses to the HIV/AIDS Crisis: a Case Study of New Juaben Municipality, Ghana', *Research Review: Institute of African Studies*, Univ. of Ghana, Vol. 22, no. 2, pp. 77-91.

This study explores how youth and youth organizations in the New Juaben municipality of Ghana's Eastern Region are tackling issues relating to youth and HIV/AIDS since 2001. In particular it examines the role of young people in HIV prevention programmes (cases of 4-H Ghana and the Philip Foundation) and looks at the obstacles facing youth in the fight against the HIV pandemic. Fieldwork was carried out in 2004. The study argues that the youth of New Juaben municipality are playing a leading role in dealing with the spread of the HIV/AIDS pandemic.

## 164.  Beard, Betty J.

2007, 'Outcomes of Community Based Orphan Care Programmes in Malawi', *Journal of Social Development in Africa*, Vol. 22, no. 1, pp. 35-52.

The primary purpose of the present study was to examine how community based orphan care programmes assess the outcomes of their activities. In this exploratory, descriptive field study, 31 programmes were visited in 2003 and in-depth interviews were conducted using open-ended questions. Four major themes emerged: pride (accomplishment), changes in children, attendance at programmes, and responses from community and outsiders. A preponderance of responses about outcomes was related to the changes observed in children as a result of programme activities. These changes included improvements in health status and educational accomplishment. Little or no written documentation is kept by community based orphan care programmes and data are primarily anecdotal. There is a tendency to focus on evaluation of process rather than outcomes.

## 165. Bray, Rachel

2003, 'Predicting the Social Consequences of Orphanhood in South Africa', *African Journal of AIDS Research*, Vol. 2, no. 1, pp. 39-55.

This paper examines and questions the predictions found in the academic and policy literature of social breakdown in southern Africa in the wake of anticipated high rates of orphanhood caused by the AIDS epidemic. Analysis of the logic underlying these predictions reveals four causal relationships necessary to fulfill such dramatic and apocalyptic predictions: high AIDS mortality rates will produce high numbers of orphans; these orphans will become children who do not live in appropriate social environments to equip them for adult citizenship; poor socialization will mean that children orphaned by AIDS will not live within society's moral codes (becoming, for example, street children or juvenile delinquents); and large numbers of such 'asocial' or 'antisocial' children will precipitate a breakdown in the social fabric. Evidence for each of these steps in the argument is scrutinized using available data from southern Africa and other regions that have moved further through the epidemic's cycle. The paper argues that such apocalyptic predictions are unfounded and ill-considered.

## 166. Daniel, Marguerite, Helen Malinga Apila and Rune Bjørge

2007, 'Breaching Cultural Silence: Enhancing Resilience Among Ugandan Orphans', *African Journal of AIDS Research*, Vol. 6, no. 2, pp. 109-120.

This paper examines the impact of cultural silence on the resilience of children orphaned by AIDS in Uganda. Cultural silence is often linked with denial. This article explores the complexities of cultural silence in terms of its causes, justifications and impacts. The findings from two small, in-depth qualitative studies (carried out in 2000-2001) among orphans who were being supported by community-based organizations in Kampala illustrate the impacts of cultural silence and disclosure on the coping ability of orphaned children. The discussion examines the findings by using a model of resilience, centred on the concepts of closeness and competence as conditions for coping.

## 167. Deffo, Modeste

2006, 'HIV/AIDS Prevention Strategies in Cameroon: Anthropological Analysis of Life Histories of People with AIDS and the Response of Youths in Schools', *The African Anthropologist*, Vol. 13, no. 1/2, pp. 26-48.

This research is grounded on the need for an innovative HIV/AIDS prevention programme targeting adolescents. The objective is to test and expand a model of AIDS education that involves People Living with HIV/AIDS (PLWHAs) as resource persons. PLWHAs were invited to share their experiences with high school students in Yaoundé. The purpose of the research was to show that narratives can be used effectively to achieve public health goals.

## 168. Doctor, Henry

2004, 'Parental Survival, Living Arrangements and School Enrolment of Children in Malawi in the Era of HIV/AIDS', *Journal of Social Development in Africa*, Vol. 19, no. 1, pp. 31-56.

Using the 1998 Malawi census data, this paper examines the level of orphanhood, the pattern of living arrangements and the effect of poverty on the school enrolment of children in Malawi during a period when adult HIV/AIDS prevalence had reached epidemic proportions. Results show that the proportion of orphans increases with age. These findings are consistent with results from other countries that are hit hard by the AIDS epidemic and point to the critical role of the extended family system in taking care of the disadvantaged and vulnerable children.

## 169. Dube, Linda and Tomaida Banda, (eds)

2006, 'Special Issue on Orphans and Other Vulnerable Children', *Journal of social development in Africa*, Vol. 21, no. 1, pp.1012-1080.

The papers in this special issue have as their broad theme issues around children's vulnerability in the face of the challenges posed by HIV and AIDS and poverty. The authors are a mix of academics, researchers and practitioners, some local, some based abroad. A key message coming through from the papers is that perhaps the most effective intervention strategy where the plight of orphans and other vulnerable children in Zimbabwe is concerned, is to help strengthen family ties and networks, and to support communities and institutions that cater for children, such as schools.

## 170. Fagbemissi, Rose C., Rico Lie and Cees Leeuwis

2009, 'Diversity and Mobility in Households with Children Orphaned by AIDS in Couffo, Benin', *African Journal of AIDS Research*, Vol. 8, no. 3, pp. 261-274.

This paper characterizes children orphaned by AIDS in the Couffo region of Benin. A 2006 census conducted for the research revealed a total of 315 such orphans, aged 0 to 14 years, within 88 households. Seventy-one percent of these children were under the care of their mothers or grandmothers, 68 percent were fatherless, 58 percent were between the ages of 7 and 12, and 68 percent were in primary school. An in-depth study of the orphans' lives, undertaken to complement the census, revealed that these orphans were highly mobile between households. Orphan mobility appeared to be a deliberate household strategy to manage orphanhood.

## 171. Francis-Chizororo, Monica

2010, 'Growing up Without Parents: Socialisation and Gender Relations in Orphaned-Child-Headed Households in Rural Zimbabwe', *Journal of Southern African Studies*, Vol. 36, no. 3, pp. 711-727.

Drawing on ethnographic research with five child heads and their siblings, this article explores how orphaned children living in 'child only' households organize themselves in terms of household domestic and paid work roles, explores the socialization of children by children and the negotiation of teenage girls' movement. Further, it examines whether the orphaned children are in some way attempting to 'mimic' previously existing family/household gender relations after parental death. The study shows that all members in the CHHs irrespective of age and gender are an integral part of household labour including food production. Although there is masculinization of domestic chores in boys 'only' households, roles are distributed by age. On the other hand, households with a gender mix tend to follow traditional gender norms. Conflict often arises when boys control teenage girls' movement and sexuality.

## 172. Harms, Sheila, Ruth Kizza, Joshua Ssebunnya, and Susan Jack

2009, 'Conceptions of Mental Health Among Ugandan Youth Orphaned by AIDS', *African Journal of AIDS Research*, Vol. 8, no. 1, pp. 7-16.

A qualitative study conducted to describe the experience of orphanhood and its impact on mental health from the culturally specific perspective of Ugandan youths. It is based on interviews with a sample of 13 youths (ages 12 to 18) who had lost one or both parents to AIDS illness and who were also affiliated with a nongovernmental organization providing support to orphans. The orphaned youths experienced significant ongoing emotional difficulties following the death of their parent(s). They were unfamiliar with the term 'mental health', however they easily identified factors associated with good or poor mental health. The findings of the study suggest that Western terminologies and symptom constellations in the American Psychiatric Association's 'Diagnostic and statistical manual of mental disorders', IV (1994) may not be applicable in an African cultural context.

## 173. Howard, Brian, Nelia Matinhure, Sheryl A. McCurdy, and Cary Alan Johnson

2006, 'Psychosocial Disadvantage: Preparation, Grieving, Remembrance and Recovery for Orphans in Eastern Zimbabwe', *African Journal of AIDS Research*, Vol. 5, no. 1, pp. 71-83.

This study describes the preparation, grief, and memorial experiences and the physical and psychosocial well-being of 144 double orphans and 109 single orphans in Mutasa District, rural eastern Zimbabwe, where a survey was carried out in 2003. Most received no preparation or orphan-specific support for mourning and emotional recovery. On measures of physical and psychosocial well-being, orphans did more poorly than 87 non-orphaned classmates, perhaps reflecting the combined interaction of economic disadvantage and orphan status. Financial hardship was most severe among single orphans. Double orphans' responses suggested perceptions of isolation, lack of support and personal difference. Distress was greatest among younger orphans (under 13 years).

### 174. Jones, Lynne

2006, 'Sexual Discourse and Decision-Making by Urban Youth in AIDS-Afflicted Swaziland', *African Journal of AIDS Research*, Vol. 5, no. 2, pp. 145-157.

This article begins by considering the ethics and practicalities of researching sensitive issues with older children and young adults in the context of HIV/AIDS. As part of qualitative fieldwork in the municipality of Mbabane, Swaziland, family caregivers and learners at two secondary schools explained how and where sexual health knowledge is gained and what they consider to be the main influences on sexual decision-making. The findings show that despite one of the highest rates of HIV infection in the world, the information reaching youth in Swaziland is still often inaccurate and confusing.

### 175. Kuhanen, Jan, Riikka Shemeikka, Veija Notkola, and Margareth Nghixulifa

2008, 'Junior-Headed Households as a Possible Strategy for Coping with the Growing Orphan Crisis in Northern Namibia', *African Journal of AIDS Research*, Vol. 7, no. 1, pp. 123-132.

The authors report research concerning junior-headed households among Oshiwambo speakers in north-central Namibia. Based on field interviews with randomly sampled junior heads of households and selected key informants, they outline some features common to the junior-headed households and the ways in which they attempt to manage their lives. The paper poses the question, do junior-headed households represent a coping strategy in a situation where the upper limits of the ability of extended families to absorb and provide care for orphans has been reached? The ability of junior heads of households to run their households and care for younger children is limited by lack of experience, unemployment, and poverty. The primary function of these juniors appears to be maintaining order and providing basic security against abuse and the grabbing of property. The authors propose that efforts be made to secure access to education for junior heads of households, and to develop ways of improving their knowledge and skills regarding both household management and income-generating activities.

## 176. Löfgren, Johanna, Josaphat Byamugisha, Per Tillgren, and Birgitta Rubenson

2009, 'The Perspectives of in-School Youths in Kampala, Uganda, on the Role of Parents in HIV Prevention', *African Journal of AIDS Research*, Vol. 8, no. 2, p. 193-200.

This qualitative study explores how young Ugandans perceive and experience the role of parents in preventing the spread of HIV among youths. Data were gathered from semi-structured face-to-face interviews with 16 in-school youths, ages 18-20, residing in Kampala. A key finding is that the youths perceived parenting styles as influencing HIV prevention among youths. The participants expressed the idea that parents can importantly contribute to preventing the spread of HIV among youths by supporting their own adolescent children and discussing topics like sex, relationships, and HIV in an age-appropriate way. The participants also described how parents treat girls and boys differently; however, no significant association was found between how girls and boys conceptualised parents' roles.

## 177. MacPhail, Catherine

2006, 'Youth-driven HIV Prevention Programmes in South Africa: Social Capital, Empowerment and Conscientisation', *Social Dynamics*, Vol. 32, no. 2, pp. 170-196.

The community-level attributes of two youth HIV prevention initiatives in a single community, a township in South Africa about an hour to the southwest of Johannesburg, are examined using the concepts of social capital, empowerment and critical consciousness. Both the school-based peer education programme and youth-initiated public clinic 'add-on' facility for the treatment of adolescent sexually transmitted diseases aimed at improving awareness and prevention and getting young people to engage in health enhancing behaviour. The two programmes had differing experiences in terms of implementation, community acceptance, sustainability and achieving their goals, and show how much more difficult it is to engage communities in social change for improved sexual health than in the provision of services. The analysis highlights the importance of ensuring adolescent agency in HIV prevention through access to power, resources and alliances, and acknowledgement of skills.

## 178. Mariya Mukhtar-Yola, Solomon Adeleke, Dayyabu Gwarzo, and Zubaida Farouk Ladan

2006, 'Preliminary Investigation of Adherence to Antiretroviral Therapy Among Children in Aminu Kano Teaching Hospital, Nigeria', *African Journal of AIDS Research*, Vol. 5, no. 2, pp. 141-144.

To determine the adherence level and the reasons for non-adherence to antiretroviral therapy (ART) among children attending the clinic for infectious diseases at Aminu Kano Teaching Hospital in Nigeria, a cross-sectional study using the self-report tool was carried out in 2005 among 40 children with HIV infection who had been on ART for at least six months. Thirty-two patients (80 percent) were 95 percent or more adherent to their medications. The most common reasons for non-adherence were running out of medicines and the inability to purchase more due to financial constraints; other barriers were non-availability and inaccessibility to medications. Eighty-five percent of the paediatric patients took their medications at the same time everyday, and scheduled appointments were kept by 87.5 percent.

## 179. Moletsane, Relebohile

2002, *What Kind of Future can we Make: Education, Youth and HIV/AIDS*, Durban, South Africa: Agenda Feminist Media.

This special issue of 'Agenda' looks at some of the issues surrounding HIV prevention strategies for young people, specifically in the school context, and focuses attention on the gendered nature of youth experience. It draws on the work of gender and HIV/AIDS activists who participated in a colloquium held in April 2002 at the University of Natal-Durban, South Africa. Contributors to the issue emphasize that youth are not a homogeneous social grouping, making it imperative that context-specific interventions are developed. Contributions deal, amongst others, with the school setting, youth culture in contemporary urban townships, gendered student identities at the University of Botswana, masculinity in HIV intervention, self-reported risk behaviour in rural KwaZulu Natal high schools, sexuality education in a girls' school in Eastern Uganda, and the current heterosexual focus of HIV/AIDS prevention campaigns.

## 180. Mtika, Mike Mathambo

2003, 'Family Transfers in a Subsistence Economy and Under a High Incidence of HIV/AIDS: the case of rural Malawi', *Journal of Contemporary African Studies*, Vol. 21, no. 1, pp. 69-92.

Based on quantitative and qualitative data from the Malawi Family Transfers research conducted in 1999, the author explores the patterns of transfers among close relatives (prime-age adults to and from their fathers, mothers, brothers, sisters, and children) in rural Malawi. The evidence suggests that prime-age adults are central to vertical or intergenerational resource transfers (resource flows upward to their parents and downward to their children) and lateral or generational resource exchanges (respondent exchanges with their brothers and sisters). The findings generally support the embodied capital investment proposition about the differential involvement in social, economic, and biological reproduction by children, the middle generation, and the old.

## 181. Mulumba, Deborah

2008, 'The Capacity of War and HIV/AIDS-Affected Households to Provide Livelihood and Protection to Orphans and Vulnerable Children in Uganda', *East African Journal of Peace & Human Rights*, Vol. 14, no. 2, pp. 423-439.

This article is derived out of research conducted in six districts in Uganda in 2005. The research findings show that far from realizing the government's aspirations of orphans being provided for by the extended family, the reality is that the family itself was vulnerable and not in a position to deliver the necessary protection and livelihoods. This placed the orphans in a precarious situation and heightened their vulnerability to abuse, poverty and other violations of their human rights.

## 182. Mushunje, Mildred T. and Muriel Mafico

2007, 'Walking the Talk: Zimbabwe's Experience in Implementing the National Action Plan for Orphans and Vulnerable Children', *Journal of Social Development in Africa*, Vol. 22, no. 2, pp. 35-62.

The authors examine Zimbabwe's experience to date with regard to implementation of PoS. They reflect on the events leading to the creation of Programme of Support (PoS), and then consider the current state of affairs in respect of the performance of this strategy. Challenges that organizations are likely to face in accessing funds from PoS are highlighted. The paper observes that notwithstanding the fact that the strategy comes with challenges and uncertainties, PoS is a new, innovative and viable approach to programming for OVC.

## 183. Muzvidziwa, Victor Ngonidzashe

2006, 'A Conceptual Framework for Research on HIV/AIDS and Orphans in Zimbabwe', *The African Anthropologist*, Vol. 13, no. 1/2, pp. 49-67

This paper presents an account of orphan care in Zimbabwe and the author's views on how research and support programmes for orphans could be handled in the country. The paper sketches a general picture of the precarious situation of orphans in Zimbabwe. The growing number of orphans in the country is a sufficient reason for policymakers to design innovative strategies to cope with the problem. The paper argues for the adoption of a livelihoods actor-oriented approach to analyse orphans' survival strategies. It examines data on orphans in Zimbabwe and finds the livelihoods actor-oriented approach quite useful. It also identifies policy gaps in the care of orphans. Even though it acknowledges the need for quantitative data, the paper posits that orphan care strategies would benefit more from the adoption of qualitative research designs.

### 184. Nshindano, Chama and Pranitha Maharaj

2008, 'Reasons for Multiple Sexual Partnerships: Perspectives of Young People in Zambia', *African Journal of AIDS Research*, Vol. 7, no. 1, pp. 37-44.

This study explores youths' perceptions of multiple sexual partnerships in the context of HIV and AIDS. The study draws on four focus group discussions and 10 in-depth interviews with university students in Lusaka, Zambia, in 2006. While the young people were generally aware of the HIV-related risk associated with multiple sexual partnerships, they felt several obstacles prevented them from changing their sexual behaviour. Of special interest are their perceptions related to socioeconomic disadvantages and cultural factors.

### 185. Nyambedha, Erick Otieno

2007, 'Vulnerability to HIV Infection Among Luo Female Adolescent Orphans in Western Kenya', *African Journal of AIDS Research*, Vol. 6, no. 3, pp. 287-295.

This paper examines the vulnerability to HIV infection of Luo female adolescent orphans in Nyang'oma division, Bondo district, western Kenya, focusing on the narrative of one 15-year-old female maternal orphan, relating her migratory life. Based on research carried out in 2004/2005, the paper considers the migratory life circumstances that can influence adolescent girls' patterns of sexual behaviour. It concludes that there is a need to look at the changes in the institution of the family, orphaned children's migration patterns, and the broader socioeconomic conditions in the lives of youth in resource-poor settings.

### 186. Nyamukapa, Constance A. Geoff Foster and Simon Gregson

2003, 'Orphans' Household Circumstances and Access to Education in a Maturing HIV epidemic in Eastern Zimbabwe'. *Journal of Social Development in Africa*, Vol. 18, no. 2, pp. 7-32.

The authors describe patterns of orphanhood and orphans' educational experience in populations in eastern Zimbabwe subject to a major HIV epidemic which is maturing into its endemic phase. Levels of orphanhood have grown recently but rates of maternal and double orphanhood, in particular, are likely to continue to increase for several years to come. Orphans are found disproportionately in rural, female, elderly and adolescent-headed households. Each of these is a risk factor for more extreme poverty. The over-representation in rural areas could reflect urban-rural migration around the time of death of the parent due to loss of income and the high cost of living in towns. Over-representation in female, elderly and adolescent-headed households reflects the predisposition of men to seek employment in towns, estates and mines; the higher level of paternal orphanhood; the reluctance of second wives to take responsibility for their predecessors' children and stress in the extended family system.

## 187. Nyasani, Evalyne, Erna Sterberg and Helen Smith

2009, 'Fostering Children Affected by AIDS in Richards Bay, South Africa: a Qualitative Study of Grandparents' Experiences', *African Journal of AIDS Research*, Vol. 8, no. 2, pp. 181-192.

This study uses qualitative research to explore the experiences of grandparents fostering children orphaned by AIDS in Richards Bay, KwaZulu-Natal Province, South Africa. The idea was born after a local HIV support organization (Richards Bay Family Care) observed a trend within their organization of grandparents increasingly becoming foster parents for orphans. An exploratory study was conducted in the organization's three target areas (two rural villages and urban Richards Bay); the ultimate aim was to explore options for improving financial and emotional support for this group. Important problems identified by the grandparents were child discipline and a feeling of disharmony in the intergenerational relationship. Government foster care grants were identified as a regular source of income for especially the rural foster care providers.

## 188. Ogunleye, Foluke

2003, 'Zimbabwe's Theatre for Young People: a Documentation of Personal Development and Social Responsibility', *Journal of Humanities: University of Malawi*, No. 17, pp. 42-61.

The activities of Zimbabwean theatre for young people are explored in case studies of Chipawo, Children's Performing Arts Workshop, an educational, nonprofit theatre established in 1989 in Harare; the National

Arts Council of Zimbabwe, a parastatal organization established in 1985 to spearhead, coordinate and facilitate the development and promotion of arts and cultural activities; the National Theatre Organization; Amakhosi, a Ndebele-based community theatre company in Bulawayo; PLAN, an international agency which uses various performance art techniques to educate children on issues such as HIV/AIDS, child abuse, teenage pregnancy, and child labour, and empower them to protect themselves; and projects initiated by MARCH, Modelling and Reinforcement to Combat HIV, which focus on the promotion of health and social issues, amongst others through social change oriented drama.

## 189. Orne-Gliemann, Joanna

2009, 'Quelle Place Pour les Hommes dans les Programmes de Prévention de la Transmission Mère-Enfant du VIH?: Revue de la Littérature et étude de cas dans les Pays en Développement', *Autrepart*, No. 52, pp. 113-129.

This study first presents a review of the literature on male involvement in prevention of mother to child transmission of HIV (PMTCT) in resource-limited countries, especially sub-Saharan Africa, and the results of a cross-sectional survey and qualitative behavior analysis carried out as part of an intervention trial project in four of these countries. Author shows that men play an important role in the acceptability and use of services to prevent mother to child transmission of HIV but finds that these services do not pay enough attention to men and taken by men is low. The lack of involvement of men is explained by three main factors: one, the conceptual and structural prevention of mother to child transmission of HIV methods that primarily focus on mother and child, two, the lack of communication between the couple, and three, the social constructions of the role of men in the reproductive sphere.

## 190. Parsitau, Damaris Seleina

2009/10, ''Keep Holy Distance and Abstain Till he Comes': Interrogating a Pentecostal Church's Engagements with HIV/AIDS and the Youth in Kenya', *Africa Today*, Vol. 56, no. 1, pp. 45-64.

The author discusses how the Deliverance Church in Kenya has attempted to provide moral solutions to the HIV/AIDS pandemic by promoting behavioral change among the youth: teaching abstinence before marriage and fidelity within marriage and requires mandatory HIV testing for those intending to get married. Such teachings confine HIV/AIDS to issues of sex, obscure the complexity of sexuality, and ignore social, economic, and political situations that fuel the spread of the virus. In this response, the church has entered into a contested moral minefield, in which it is attempting socially and sexually to discipline its members, particularly its youthful constituency. These messages reach many young people, who form the bulk of the membership of this church. Many strive to follow the church's teachings, but do not accept them uncritically, and some refuse to be morally disciplined by them.

### 191. Paruk, Zubeda, Inge Petersen and Arvin Bhana

2009, 'Facilitating Health-Enabling Social Contexts for Youth: Qualitative Evaluation of a Family-Based HIV-Prevention Pilot Programme', *African Journal of AIDS Research*, Vol. 8, no. 1, pp. 61-68.

This paper reports on a post-intervention qualitative evaluation of the pilot intervention of the AmaQhawe Family Project, in South Africa, which is a cartoon-based, manualized intervention delivered to multiple family groups over 10 sessions, aimed at preventing HIV in adolescents through strengthening the adult protective shield. Semi-structured interviews with nine women who had participated in the pilot intervention were used to understand participants' perceptions of how the family-based HIV-prevention programme had assisted in addressing the issues identified in a pre-intervention exploratory study. The findings indicate that at an individual level, the women interviewed had experienced an improved sense of empowerment, both as parents and as women. They also reported increased social support for effective parenting. At a collective level, the women reported that the programme had helped them to exert better informal social controls within the community, as well as to increase their social leverage and participation in community organizations. The findings suggest that HIV interventions involving families can strengthen the adult protective shield to facilitate health-enabling social contexts for youth.

## 192. Pharoah, Robyn, (ed.)

2004, *A Generation at Risk?: HIV/AIDS, Vulnerable Children and Security in Southern Africa*, Institute for Security Studies.

This collective volume focuses on children left orphaned and vulnerable by HIV/AIDS in Southern Africa. The authors share different examples of the increasingly significant humanitarian and developmental concerns caused by HIV/AIDS, security issues, the well-being of individuals, households, communities, and states. By reducing the financial and emotional resources available to children, causing trauma and alienation and effectively limiting the realistic aspirations of the youngsters affected, some contributors argue that the epidemic may create generations of disenfranchised and potentially dysfunctional young people who lack the socialisation necessary for constructive social engagement. Others show that growing numbers of marginalised children may in turn impact on stability and security in at least two ways: they may become both the victims and perpetrators of crime; and may provide a ready recruitment pool for individuals and organisations wishing to challenge the existing status quo.

## 193. Samson, Michael J.

2002, 'HIV/AIDS and Poverty in Households with Children Suffering from Malnutrition: the Role of Social Security in Mount Frere'. *The South African Journal of Economics*, Vol. 70, no. 7, pp. 1148-1172.

This study is based on interviews with 26 households in 2001 and explores how HIV/AIDS and other long-term chronic illnesses, together with extreme poverty, affect households with children suffering from severe malnutrition. It examines the role of social security in supporting or failing to support these households as they cope with the impact of HIV/AIDS. The most consistent finding is the extent to which extremely poor households depend on remittances and social security. But targeting mechanisms, the means test and bureaucratic impediments to grant delivery undermine the effectiveness of the existing system of social protection.

## 194.  Shaw, Stacey A. and Jini L. Roby

2007, 'Child Welfare Perspectives of Caregivers Raising Orphans and Vulnerable Children in Uganda', *Journal of Social Development in Africa*, Vol. 22, no. 2, pp. 9-34.

Believing that the voices of the caregivers responsible for raising orphans are of great value in determining priorities and practical solutions for orphan care, the researchers interviewed 315 caregivers in 2005 in Uganda who were raising orphans and other vulnerable children. The study found that caregivers placed responsibility for the orphan crisis on the HIV/AIDS pandemic, and stressed the importance of HIV/AIDS education in helping countries reduce numbers of orphans in the future. Caregivers reported feeling that many groups (including relatives, community members, governments and international programmes) have extensive obligations for helping children, and expressed views on legal, in-country and international adoption.

## 195.  Shobo, Yetunde

2007, 'Youth's Perceptions of HIV Infection Risk: a Sex-Specific Test of Two Risk Models', *African Journal of AIDS Research*, Vol. 6, no. 1, pp. 1-8.

This study examines the associations between the cumulative and additive risk models and Nigerian youth's likelihood of perceiving vulnerability to HIV infection. Both models of risk seem to provide unique contributions to such understanding. The analysis is based on data from the 2003 Demographic and Health Survey in Nigeria. The model of additive risk revealed that having had a sexually transmitted disease was associated with males' perceptions of vulnerability to HIV infection, whereas past sexual activity and having had multiple sexual partners were linked to females' perceptions of vulnerability. These sex-specific findings are highly relevant for HIV prevention and intervention programmes for youth in sub-Saharan Africa.

## 196. Simpson, Barbara and Tanusha Raniga

2004, 'Co-Housing as a Possible Housing Option for Children Affected by HIV/AIDS: Evidence from Informal Settlements', *Urban Forum*, Vol. 15, no. 4, pp. 365-379.

This paper suggests that co-housing offers a form of housing that could contribute to a more supportive environment that could absorb orphaned children more easily than the existing model of single family dwellings. Co-housing is the name for a type of voluntary, collaborative housing that has been developing in Denmark, the USA and Australia since the 1970s. This type of housing scheme combines the autonomy of private dwellings with the advantages of community living. Co-housing builds on family values and takes into account the caring, nurturing and supportive responsibilities of communities as a whole. The paper is based on an exploratory study, which examined the perceptions of community leaders in four urban and rural informal settlements in KwaZulu-Natal - Etete, Seatides informal, Bayview informal and Lusaka - regarding the impact of HIV/AIDS on living arrangements.

## 197. Singhal, Arvind and W. Stephen Howard, (eds)

2003, *The Children of Africa Confront AIDS: from Vulnerability to Possibility*, Athens: Ohio University Press.

This edited volume depicts the reality of how African children deal with the AIDS epidemic, and how the discourse of their vulnerability affects acts of coping and courage. It highlights such issues as democracy, sexual violence, psychological and emotional needs, participatory interventions, using community radio for behavior change, and children and civil conflict in the context of HIV/AIDS.

## 198. Stergaard, Lise Rosendal and Helle Samuelsen

2004, 'Muted Voices: HIV/AIDS and the Young people of Burkina Faso and Senegal', *African Journal of AIDS Research*, Vol. 3, no. 2, pp. 103-112.

This article explores the discrepancies between the vocal public discourse on HIV/AIDS and sexuality as generally encouraged by policymakers and donor communities in Africa, the often hushed voices of their target groups: young people in African communities. Based on fieldwork carried out 2002 and 2003 among urban youth in Senegal and Burkina Faso, it describes the silence of young people with regard to HIV/AIDS and sexuality as a social phenomenon, focusing on family relations, peer relations and gender aspects in partnerships.

## 199. Townsend, Loraine and Andy Dawes

2004, 'Willingness to Care for Children Orphaned by HIV/AIDS: a Study of Foster and Adoptive Parents', *African Journal of AIDS Research*, Vol. 3, no. 1, pp. 69-80.

The present study explores the willingness of adoptive and foster parents to care for a child orphaned by HIV/AIDS. Although some differences were noted depending on the HIV status of the child and whether the respondent was an adoptive or foster parent, results indicate an overall willingness in these populations to care for children orphaned by HIV/AIDS. The evidence also suggests that HIV-negative female orphans who are younger than 6 years, and who are family members, or from the same cultural background as the potential caregivers and do not have surviving relatives or siblings, have the best chance of being taken into foster or adoptive care.

## 200. Van Graan, Anneke Engela Van der Walt and Mada Watson

2007, 'Community-Based Care of Children with HIV in Potchefstroom, South Africa', *African Journal of AIDS Research*, Vol. 6, no. 3, pp. 305-313.

The present authors investigate the extent of nonprofessional caregivers' knowledge and needs, specifically those within the Potchefstroom district of the North-West Province. The objectives include formulating guidelines for a training programme that can enhance relevant knowledge and skills among these caregivers. Quantitative data were gathered using a questionnaire, which was developed following a literature study. The 109 nonprofessional caregivers who responded to the questionnaire displayed some knowledge and skills concerning specifically the care of children with HIV or AIDS, although gaps existed concerning their knowledge of community-based referral, caring needs specific to children, and precautionary measures to prevent HIV transmission. Recommendations are made with specific reference to a training programme.

## 201. Wyss, Susi, J. Ablordeppey, J. Okrah, and A. Kyei

2007, 'Reaching Disenfranchised Youth and Mobile Populations in Ghana Through Voluntary Counselling and Testing Services for HIV', *African Journal of AIDS Research.*, Vol. 6, no. 2, pp. 121-128

This paper documents the evaluation of a 20-month project (2003-2005) to provide voluntary counselling and testing (VCT) to a mobile population of youth surrounding the Agbogbloshie market in Accra, Ghana. The specific objectives of the evaluation were to determine to what extent targets for providing VCT services to the specified populationwere reached; how HIV prevalence among clients compared to that of the general population; to what extent former clients self-reported behaviour change; and whether useful lessons could be drawn regarding fees, hours, and location of services, as well as use of peer educators to increase use of VCT services among the target population. Various methodologies, including questionnaires, focus group discussions, a review of the service statistics and an exit poll of clients were used to evaluate the project. The evaluation stressed the need to appropriately remunerate peer educators for their work whenever possible.

## 202. Zisser, Alison and Dennis Francis

2006, 'Youth Have a New Attitude on AIDS, but are They Talking About it?' *African Journal of AIDS Research*, Vol. 5, no. 2, pp. 189-196.

The authors examine youths' understanding and communication habits surrounding the 'Get Attitude' print campaign of loveLife, the largest HIV/AIDS awareness movement in South Africa to date. Intrigued by the ambiguous campaign message, they implemented a questionnaire-based study in three urban KwaZulu-Natal schools to investigate how youth are interpreting the images and to determine whether they would connect the personality-aimed message with HIV prevention. The study was largely exploratory, with the data revealing that the youth did interpret the images as intended by loveLife. While the campaign failed to stimulate discussion for many of the youth, those who did talk about the campaign were more likely to speak to their teachers than to parents or friends.

# Part VIII

## Media, Popular Culture, and Representation

## 203. Adogame, Afe

2006, 'The 419 Code as business unusual: the Advance Fee Fraud online discourse', *International Journal of Humanistic Studies*, Vol. 5, pp. 54-72.

This paper examines the advent and consolidation of AFF in the mid-1980s, and shows how, with the expansion of Advance Fee Fraud (a.k.a. '419') online, a cross-section of Nigerian youth increasingly engage the new media as a gateway to economic empowerment. Through an analysis of over 150 scam e-letters, randomly selected from some thousand collected between January 2002 and October 2003, the paper highlights the emerging variations of a theme. What began as a relatively simple adaptation of a traditional advance fee ploy has developed into an extensive criminal operation with links to other crimes internationally. At the local level, the Nigerian government has embarked upon a range of preventive measures, including education of consumers as to the risks involved in replying to AFF letters. But the problem is no longer one for Nigeria or West Africa alone to deal with as it has taken on a truly transnational character.

## 204. Akyeampong, Emmanuel

2002, 'Drinking with Friends: Popular Culture, the Working Poor, and Youth Drinking in Independent Ghana', *Alcohol in Africa: mixing business, pleasure, and politics*, ed., Deborah Fahy Bryceson, Portsmouth, NH: Heinemann: pp. 215-230.

This chapter follows from observations made by the author during fieldwork in Kumasi (Ghana) in 1992 among youth on drinking patterns and leisure where he was struck by the celebration of hard drinking. The chapter examines contemporary drinking patterns among youth in the working-class area of Roman Hill, near Kumasi's Central Market in which teenagers hoped to become successful traders but have been unsuccessful. The author concludes that having been forced into premature adulthood and into being self-sufficient, youth have used drink as a balm to sooth the indignities of poverty, unemployment and insecurity

## 205. Arnoldi, Mary Jo

2005/06, 'Youth Festivals and Museums: the Cultural Politics of Public Memory in Postcolonial Mali', *Africa Today*, Vol. 52, no. 4, pp. 55-76.

This paper argues that public memory practices are essentially political, and in postcolonial Mali, as elsewhere in Africa, the State's cultural agenda has involved a refocusing and revalorization of the precolonial past through both performance and material culture and shows how in postcolonial Mali, youth arts and sports festivals and the National Museum have been important sites for constructing a national culture. The State has appropriated traditional performing arts into youth festivals through the use of different media, and subsequently marshalled a constellation of historical memories, symbolic forms, and cultural practices in the service of this nationalist project.

## 206. Becker, Heike and Nceba Dastile

2008, 'Global and African: Exploring Hip-Hop Artists in Philippi Township, Cape Town', *Anthropology Southern Africa*, Vol. 31, no. 1/2, pp. 20-29.

This article investigates hip hop, identity and global cultural flows among young people in contemporary Cape Town. It is based on ethnographic research undertaken in 2005 and focuses on hip hop performers who rap in an African language. The use of African languages in hip hop has given rise to the concept of 'spaza' hip hop, 'spaza' being the term used in South Africa for the unlicensed tuck shops set up by township residents during the apartheid era in order to challenge the economic disenfranchisement of black people.

## 207. Bjerk, Paul

2005, ''Building a New Eden': Lutheran Church Youth Choir Performances in Tanzania', *Journal of Religion in Africa*, Vol. 35, no. 3, pp. 324-361.

This is a study of three songs by a Tanzanian youth choir that reveals a synthesis of historical and intellectual sources ranging from precolonial social philosophy to Lutheran theology to Nyerere's 'ujamaa' socialism. The Ipogoro Youth Choir, in Iringa, in Tanzania's Southern Highlands, uses the voice granted to them as a church choir to argue for a national ideology that draws both pre-Christian local concepts and modern government priorities and enfolds them into a new Christian theology in which youth, as youth, have an important responsibility in society. Using the resonant pre-Christian cultural memories, the choir argues for the reestablishment of social structures that were destroyed by the colonial State. In appropriating an active role in shaping Christian ideology, the choir members reinterpret its theology into something wholly new and uniquely Tanzanian.

## 208. Bradbury, Marina

2010, 'Negotiating Identities: Representations of Childhood in Senegalese Cinema', *Journal of African Media Studies*, Vol. 2, no. 1, pp. 9-24.

This article offers a critique of reductive paradigms that pit 'the West' against 'Africa' by means of specific analysis of representations of childhood in early and contemporary Senegalese fiction films, in particular 'Afrique sur Seine' (Vieyra and Sarr, 1955), 'La noire de...' (Sembene, 1966), 'Touki Bouki/The journey of the hyena' (Mambety, 1973), 'Un amour d'enfant' (Diogaye Beye, 2004) and 'Petite lumière (Gomis, 2003). The article discusses to what extent audiovisual African representations of childhood allow African directors to reclaim autonomous yet hybrid identities on behalf of Africans, and argues that cinematic representations of childhood are key to building a more positive, multifaceted vision of Africa, African cultures and African identities.

## 209. Burgess, Thomas

2002, 'Cinema, Bell Bottoms, and Miniskirts: Struggles over Youth and Citizenship in Revolutionary Zanzibar', *The International Journal of African Historical Studies*, Vol. 35, no. 2/3, pp. 287-313.

This article argues that as political leaders sought to construct a revolutionary society, they provoked conflict with young people whose appearance was not sufficiently recognizable as African, socialist or Muslim. It discusses how nation-building as an ideology lost meaning in a deteriorating urban environment where young people in particular lacked 'productive' work. In this context Western cinema emerged as a primary escape, as well as an inspiration for clothing styles. The article then examines the reasons why the new fashions provoked official anxieties. Finally, it describes how the ruling party mobilized against unsanctioned styles in order to defend revolutionary concepts of visual order, discipline and citizenship.

## 210. Cazenave, Odile

2005, 'Writing the Child, Youth, and Violence into the Francophone Novel from sub-Saharan Africa: the Impact of Age and Gender', *Research in African Literatures*, Vol. 36, no. 2, pp. 59-71.

This article explores the question of how women and men think about and represent the child, youth, and violence in francophone African literature today. This focus was initially sparked by the observation of two concurrent features in the novel of the past decade: 1) the re-emergence of the child character or/and child voice within a new context, that of violence, and 2) the prevalence of representations of female youth within a violent postcolonial urban landscape. This observation triggered further questions: why and how children are now portrayed as directly part of a process of violence and, at times, were the voices of violence; why women writers seem to focus on youth and violence. The author explores various answers to these questions.

## 211. Drame, Mamadou

2009, Poetry Slam: A New Form of Youth's Expression Half-way Between Rap and Traditional Poetry, *CODESRIA Bulletin*, Nos 3 & 4, pp. 28-32.

Through a comparative analysis of slam poetry and rap in Senegal, this article discusses the relationship between different musical styles and traditional oral performances. The author argues that slam is an oral style based on improvisation, speech democratisation and urban expression, which brings together rap and African traditional poetry.

## 212. Englert, Birgit

2010, 'In Need of Connection: Reflections on Youth and the Translation of Film in Tanzania', *Stichproben*, Jg. 10, Nr. 18, S. 137-159.

This essay focuses on the transformation of films translated into Kiswahili from English, Hindi/Urdu, or Chinese in order to be consumed by their predominantly youthful Tanzanian audience. The author discusses the processes and shows how the films are shaped by the work of translators ('watafsiri'), but also by the people who work in the video parlours ('vibanda vya video'), the places where these films are usually consumed. The essay is based on field research in Masasi (Mtwara region) and Nachingwea (Lindi region) in February 2009 and in Dar es Salaam, Morogoro (Morogoro region) and Bagamoyo (Tanga region) in September 2009.

## 213. Englert, Birgit

2008, 'Ambiguous Relationships: Youth, Popular Music and Politics in Contemporary Tanzania', *Stichproben*, Jg. 8, Nr. 14, S. 71-96.

In this article the author argues that it is not so much the critical lyrics of some of the songs in Tanzania's music genre 'Bongo Flava', which have helped make it popular, but rather the successes of musicians in conveying self-consciousness to young people who experience that they can achieve more than hitherto thought. In this sense 'Bongo Flava' has helped provide the background for the emergence of young, charismatic personalities such as Amina Chifupa and Zitto Kabwe, who became Members of Parliament after the elections in 2005. They have started to challenge the conventional, hierarchical ways of Tanzanian politics, which used to be dominated by the older generation. The article further outlines how young 'underground' musicians perceive contemporary Tanzanian politics and how this influences their own strategies in musical production.

## 214. Ferrari, Aurelia

2007, 'Hip-Hop in Nairobi: Recognition of an International Movement and the Main Means of Expression for the Youth in Poor Residential Areas', in *Songs and Politics in Eastern Africa*, ed. by Kimani Njogu and Herve Maupeu, Dar es Salaam, Mkuki na Nyota Press, pp. 107-128.

This chapter starts by reconstructing Nairobi's hip-hop history and its ideas using the experiences of two hip-hop groups — Kalamashaka and

Mau Mau Camp — to explain the current hip-hop situation and the major difficulties they experience. The author then analyzes lyrics from 25 songs as well as from interviews with musicians from these two groups and concludes that hip-hop is an indispensable tool for understanding youth life in Nairobi.

## 215. Fusaschi, Michela

2010, 'Victimes à Tout Jamais: les Enfants et les Femmes d'Afrique: Rhétoriques de la Pitié et Humanitarisme Spectacle', *Cahiers d'études africaines*, Vol. 50, cah. 198/200, pp. 1033-1053.

The author analyzes advertising campaigns of two Italian NGOs — the first operates in the field of international adoption and campaigns for children African sorcerers and the second fights for the rights of women against female circumcision. The intention is to show how these organizations construct a representation of an 'African humanity', now adrift, consisting almost exclusively of women and children. For the NGOs, the survival of these women and children, both here and there, is totally dependent on their actions inspired by an ideology of pedagogical-morality. In this sense, the discourse on Africa available in the media in Italy is strictly related to an internal policy against Otherness - migration - and some political 'hot' topics such as the family and the role of women, adoption, sexual choices, civil rights, etc.

## 216. Githiora, Chege, (ed.)

2008, *East African culture, language and society*, Abingdon: Taylor & Francis. This edited volume explores new and emerging trends in popular culture, its nexus with language, politics and creative productions in Kenya and Tanzania, including such topics as Swahili advertising in Nairobi: innovation and language shift; Sexism and (mis)representation of women in Sheng; Keeping it real: reality and representation in Maasai hip-hop; 'Kuchanganyachanganya': topic and language choices in Tanzanian youth culture; 'Made in Riverwood': (dis)locating identities and power through Kenyan pop music; Kenyan gospel soundtracks: crossing boundaries, mapping audiences; Recreating discourse and performance in Kenyan urban space through 'mugithi', hip hop and 'gicandi'; and Clothing and the changing identities of Tanganyikan urban youths, 1920s-1950s.

## 217. Hron, Madelaine

2008, "'Ora na-azu nwa': the Figure of the Child in Third-Generation Nigerian Novels', *Research in African Literatures*, Vol. 39, no. 2, pp. 27-48. This article examines the complex role of the child or youth protagonist, who features prominently in third-generation Nigerian fiction. Countering reductionist claims that demote these texts to juvenile fiction, it draws on African, Nigerian, and children's literary criticism to argue that the hybrid space of childhood enables writers to address themes that may, in fact, be too large for adult fiction, while also engaging culturally uninformed Western readers. Focusing on the language, perspective, and agency of the child-hero, this article investigates three texts - Chimamanda Ngozi Adichie's 'Purple Hibiscus' (2004), Helen Oyeyemi's 'The Icarus Girl' (2005), and Uzodinma Iweala's 'Beasts of No Nation' (2005) - which reflect the prevailing trends in contemporary Nigerian writing: those criticizing neocolonial Nigeria, those problematizing the transnational space of diaspora, and those raising awareness about human rights violations stemming from globalization.

## 218. Ignatowski, Clare A.

2004, 'Making Ethnic Elites: Ritual, Poetics in a Cameroonian Lyce'e', *Africa: Journal of the International African Institute*, Vol. 74, no. 3, pp. 411-432. This case study of youth cultural production in Cameroon examines how lyce'e students introduce idioms of tradition and the ancestral past into the lyce'e context by creating a club modelled on a dance society popular in the region. This paper explores the meanings, functions, and effects of the creation of the 'Gurna Club by students in the Lyce'e de Doukoula, by examining students Youth Day dance performances, vibrant song discourse, and nostalgia for earlier forms of indigenous socialization (e.g. the 'gurna', youth initiation, wrestling). By inserting the communal poetics of the 'gurna' into the lycee, Tupuri youth seek to yoke multiple facets of their identity, making visible their desire to be 'gurna', even as they pursue their civic obligations as students. In creating the Gurna Club, students begin to participate in an increasing trend in Cameroon toward the use of idioms of parochialism (such as ethnically based elite associations) as strategies for garnering national power and recognition.

## 219. Kaschula, Russell H.

2007, 'Identity in the Siyagruva Series of Novels: Toward an Intercultural Literary Discourse', *Tydskrif vir Letterkunde*, Jg. 44, nr. 2, pp. 74-88.

This article explores the notion of changing South African youth identity and how it is depicted in the Siyagruva (We are Grooving) Series of novels for young adults. The article highlights the need for a broadening of literary theory in order to include an appropriate theoretical approach for new South African youth literature. This theory explores intercultural literary discourse by making use of, for example, the work of intercultural theorists such as Ting-Toomey (1999), Gudykunst (2003) and others. It is argued that this form of literary discourse is now appropriate as a theoretical paradigm within multilingual South Africa where intercultural communication is becoming a reality. The article concentrates on selected novels, though reference is also made to many of the twenty-three published novels in the Siyagruva Series, twenty in English and three translated into Xhosa.

## 220. Kiyimba, Abasi

2005, 'Gendering Social Destiny in the Proverbs of the Baganda: Reflections on Boys and Girls Becoming Men and Women', *Journal of African Cultural Studies*. Vol. 17, no. 2, pp. 253-270.

This article examines the portrayal of boys and girls in the oral literature, notably proverbs, of the Baganda of Uganda. It assesses the near-indelible impressions that oral literature creates, and how they impact on gender relations. In particular, it looks at the way these impressions lay down rules of social behaviour that determine how boys and girls eventually view each other as wives, husbands, parents, political leaders and owners of resources. The main argument of the article is that the unequally gendered relationships among the Baganda have their foundation in early childhood.

## 221. Kruger, Haidee

2007, 'Towards a Paradigm for the Study of the Translation of Children's Literature in the South African Educational Context: Some Reflections', *Language Matters*. Vol. 38, no. 2, pp. 275-298.

This article sets out some considerations for a study of the translation of children's literature in the South African educational context. It briefly focuses on the uses and functions of children's books, particularly in terms of education, before proceeding to some of the key issues that have shaped academic discourse surrounding the translation of children's literature and a brief overview of available research, focusing particularly on South Africa. The review shows that research on South African children's literature, notably in Afrikaans and English, is on the rise, but research on the translation of children's literature appears to be in a nascent stage, despite the increasing availability of translated children's texts, particularly in the indigenous languages. The article concludes with some considerations and suggestions for the construction of a theoretical framework from within which to approach the study of the translation of children's literature in the South African educational context.

## 222. Mchakulu, Japhet Ezra July

2007, 'Youth Participation in Radio Listening Clubs in Malawi', *Journal of Southern African Studies*, Vol. 33, no. 2, pp. 251-265.

This article reports on a qualitative research study that used community radio and radio listening clubs to examine the involvement of youth in community debate in Malawi. The study sample was chosen from young members of radio listening clubs in Mangochi district in Malawi's southern region. Research topics included the radio listening clubs' mode of operation in relation to community radio, the issues dominating discussion in each radio listening club and youths' experiences of constraints placed on debate. Findings suggest that community radio and its associated radio listening clubs have together created an emerging public sphere for the local community, including a space for youths and other disadvantaged groups to discuss solutions to local socioeconomic problems.

## 223. Moyer, Eileen

2005 'Street-Corner Justice in the Name of Jah: Imperatives for Peace Among Dar es Salaam Street Youth', *Africa Today*, Vol. 51, no. 3, pp. 31-58.

By taking a close look at internal peacekeeping strategies employed by a group of approximately 100 informal economy entrepreneurs on a specific street corner ('maskani') located in the middle of the central business district of Dar es Salaam, the article demonstrates that such questions are best answered from a local perspective. While Marley's global appeal may be attributed to shared experiences of inequality, the ways this popularity emerges locally sheds light on the particularities of those experiences. Many 'wamaskani' who promoted social ideals of peaceful coexistence, cloaked in Rastafari philosophy, did so to promote a better quality of life in the context of their daily negotiations with others who worked at the corner.

## 224. Mwaura, Bantu

2007, 'Kenyan Youth and the Entropic Destruction of a Hopeful Social Order' in *Cultural production and social change in Kenya: building bridges*, ed. by Kimani Njogu and G. Oluoch-Olunya, Nairobi: Twaweza Communications, pp. 63-74.

This chapter critiques the role of youth in the contemporary Kenya's social order arguing that sometimes youth are to blame for their own predicament as they fail to harness the opportunities provided them by society. The author also presents the other side of the story arguing that society has been unable to support innovations by youth especially those that challenge received social wisdom.

## 225. Ndlovu, Musa

2008, 'South African Journalism and Mass Communication Research on Youth and News Media: a Reflection', *Ecquid Novi*, Vol. 29, no. 1, pp. 64-78.

This study explores conceptual and methodological frameworks through which the relationship between South African youth and news media has been investigated. It concentrates primarily on the exploration and framing of the youth-news media relationship; the choice of media; the construction of youth identity; and preferred research methodologies and theoretical approaches. The investigation is contextualized within ontological, epistemological, and political-ideological debates in local JMCS, and in global discourses on youth and news media. The study concludes that post-1994 local studies largely adopted qualitative research methods, critical social theory, and cultural studies, rather than socialization and functionalist theories.

## 226. Ntarangwi, Mwenda

2009, *East African Hip Hop: Youth Culture and Globalization*, Urbana, IL: University of Illinois Press.

Analyzes youth in East Africa using hip hop to enter into public political and economic spaces amid global changes and processes. Using ethnographic data from Kenya, Uganda and Tanzania the author analyzes how East African youth encounter and make sense of lived and imagined experiences within global economic and political structures, showing how youth create spaces through which they enter a public domain that often excludes them in favor of those who wield social, political, and economic power. The main argument is that hip hop acts as an alternative prism through which youth engage with globalization showing how it is on the one hand a force that replicates unequal structural, economic and political relations that the West has had with Africa, and on the other a force that creates opportunities for youth to enter into the public space and make some gainful economic and socio-cultural critique.

## 227. Nyamnjoh, Francis B. and Ben Page

2002, "'Whiteman Kontri' and the Enduring Allure of Modernity Among Cameroonian Youth', *African Affairs*, Vol. 101, no. 405, pp. 607-634.

This article gathers together representations of whiteness constructed by young black Cameroonians. It contributes to arguments about white identity by arguing that the meaning of whiteness is, in part, made by Africans. It assembles descriptions of white people and of the 'whiteman kontri' (the West) that are often contradictory and that include both positive and negative judgements. In this respect these ideas reflect both Cameroonian politics and Cameroonian identity. The authors contribute to debates about Occidentalism by suggesting that this is a concept that should be used with caution, since by suggesting an equivalent to 'Orientalism' it suggests equality and endorses an essentialized notion of whiteness and blackness, which can undermine attempts to understand the history of relations between Africa and the West.

### 228. Ogechi, Nathan Oyori

2007, 'Building Bridges Through Trichotomous youth Identities in Kenya: Evidence from Code-Choice', in *Cultural production and social change in Kenya: building bridges*, ed. by Kimani Njogu and G. Oluoch-Olunya. Nairobi: Twaweza Communications, pp. 129-147.

The author illustrates in this chapter how youth in Kenya build bridges in their language use, arguing that youth are stakeholders in reversing the polarized political and inter-ethnic relations in the country. Given the strong bond between language and identity, the author further argues that the prevailing triglossia found in Kenya is closely associated with trichotomous identities that are projected not only through grammatically stable codes and code switching but also through grammatically unstable ones. The author concludes that there is need to appreciate the trichotomous identities of code choice in weaving a true national identity among youth and by extension all Kenyans.

### 229. Odhiambo, Tom

2007, 'Juvenile Delinquency and Violence in the Fiction of Three Kenyan Writers', *Tydskrif vir Letterkunde*, Jg. 44, nr. 2, pp. 134-148.

This essay is a preliminary examination of crime and violence in postcolonial Kenyan fiction. It examines how three Kenyan writers – John Kiriamiti, Meja Mwangi and John Kigia Kimani – have dealt with the themes of crime and violence in their works 'My life in crime' (1984), 'Kill me quick' (1973), and 'Life and times of a bank robber' (1989). The article postulates that the prevalence of juvenile delinquency and the related acts of violence in these works could be read as indicators of the failure of the postcolonial State to 'include' urban youth in the mainstream of society. The essay further argues that there is a correlation between the marginalization of youth in society and their adoption of antisocial behaviour as a strategy to access material resources.

## 230. Pecora, Norma, Enyonam Osei-Hwere and Ulla Carlsson, (ed.)

2008, *African Media, African Children*, Göteborg: NORDICOM, The International Clearinghouse on Children, Youth and Media.

This tenth yearbook of the International Clearinghouse on Children, Youth and Media, focuses on the world of children's media in Africa. It includes a comparative African country report on the state of children's media in Subsaharan Africa and an agenda for meaningful research on children's agency in Africa in the context of media globalization. Specific case studies deal with the South African Broadcasting Corporation's programming for children; Islamic media for children in Senegal, Sudan and Nigeria; the content of South African television fiction for children; Ethiopian children's reception of Walt Disney animation and cartoon films; digital literacy in marginal school settings in South Africa; the production and broadcast of youth radio shows initiated by Plan West Africa; media education and child participation in radio in Ghana; community-based youth video as a tool for building democratic dialogue in South Africa; Egyptian children's experience with cyber space and the impact of virtual socialization; and children's television programmes in Ghana, South Africa, Kenya, Zambia and Zimbabwe.

## 231. Perullo, Alex

2004/05, 'Hooligans and Heroes: Youth Identity and Hip-hop in Dar es Salaam, Tanzania', *Africa Today*, Vol. 51, no. 4, pp. 75-101.

In this article, the author examines the ways that youth use rap music to confront stereotypes of young people, and reach the broader listening public through politically and socially relevant lyrics ('ujumbe mkali', 'strong messages'). Using transcriptions of lyrics and interviews with artists, the author argues that youth have turned a foreign musical form into a critical medium of social empowerment whereby they are able to create a sense of community among other urban youth, voice their ideas and opinions to a broad listening public, and alter conceptions of youth as hooligans.

## 232. Prestholdt, Jeremy

2009, 'The afterlives of 2Pac: imagery and alienation in Sierra Leone and beyond', *Journal of African Cultural Studies*, Vol. 21, no. 2, pp. 197-218.

Taking a multidisciplinary approach that weaves social history, cultural studies and globalization studies, this paper highlights the convergence of socioeconomic alienation and media proliferation since the early 1990s. It argues that this confluence has given rise to new global heroes such as Tupac, icons that have become components of a planetary symbolic lingua franca that has yet to gain significant analytical attention. The paper outlines the transnational import of Tupac by considering young combatants' evocations of him during the Sierra Leone civil war (1991-2002).

## 233. Seekings, Jeremy

2006, 'Beyond Heroes and Villains: the Rediscovery of the Ordinary in the Study of Childhood and Adolescence in South Africa', *Social Dynamics*, Vol. 32, no. 1, pp. 1-20.

This article gives an overview of research on childhood and adolescence in South Africa in the 1980s, 1990s and early 2000s especially how children have been represented. Author argues that writing about young people in South Africa in the 1980s and early 1990s was dominated by representations of them as either the 'heroes' or 'villains' of political struggle. During the political transition, young people attracted a rush of attention as the source of a series of supposed social 'problems'. In South Africa, as in other parts of Africa, children are growing up in a period of rapid social and economic change, amidst continuing urbanization, deagrarianization and educational expansion, changing households and kin relationships, new economic opportunities and prospects, and cultural globalization. This as the author argues calls for new ways of representing children.

## 234. Simone, AbdouMaliq

2008, 'Some Reflections on Making Popular Culture in Urban Africa', *African Studies Review*, Vol. 51, no. 3, pp. 75-89.

Rather than treating popular culture as some distinctive sector, this article investigates the popular as methods of bringing together activities and actors that on the surface would not seem compatible, and as experimental forms of generating value in the everyday life of urban residents. This investigation, sited largely in Douala, Cameroon, looks at how youth from varying neighbourhoods attempt to get by, and at the unexpected forms of contestation that can ensue.

## 235. Sissao, Alain-Joseph

2009, *Émergence de la Littérature D'enfance et de Jeunesse au Burkina Faso: état des Lieux, Dynamique et Avenir*, Paris: L'Harmattan.

This book is the result of work by a multidisciplinary team of Specialists in literature, linguists, and a socio-linguist and an ethno-linguist from Burkina Faso. The contributions are grouped into four parts: 1) Taking stock of literature for children in Burkina Faso, 2) Analysis of the literature of children in Burkina Faso, 3) The novel and childhood, and 4) Interview with Ansomwin Ignace Hien directed by Alain Joseph Sissao.

## 236. Siziba, Gugulethu

2009, 'Redefining the Production and Reproduction of Culture in Zimbabwe's Urban Space: The Case of Urban Grooves', *CODESRIA Bulletin*, Nos 3 & 4, pp. 19-28.

In this paper focusing on a new genre of music called 'urban grooves' in Zimbabwe the author argues that there is the need for a new and alternative discourse on culture that acknowledges the contribution of young people in the generation of Africa's reality, and one that also acknowledges that culture is much broader than a single, one-dimensional perspective of the adult world. Using song texts from urban grooves the author shows how young people re-craft a new urban and social reality that is not controlled by the state or adult cultural brokers.

## 237. Wa-Mungai, Mbugua

2007, "Is Marwa!' It's Ours': Popular Music and Identity Politics in Kenyan Youth Culture', in *Cultural Production and Social Change in Kenya: Building Bridges*, ed. by Kimani Njogu and G. Oluoch-Olunya, Nairobi: Twaweza Communications, pp. 47-62.

Author discusses the various ways youth in Kenya are using popular music to craft their identities and reframe traditional identities that were once assumed dead. Analysing a selection of music that was popular in the late 90s and early 2000s.

## 238. Wisdome, J. Tettey

2008, 'Globalization and Internet Fraud in Ghana: Interrogating the Political Economy of Survival, Subaltern Agency, and their Ramifications'. In Joseph Mensah(ed.), *Neoliberalism and Globalization in Africa: Contestations on the Embattled Continent*, New York: Palgrave Macmillan, pp. 241-266.

The author examines cyber fraud in Ghana in the context of growing assumption that such 'borderless' activities are emanating from West Africa. He notes that there is growth in Ghanaians with access to the Internet as the proliferation of cyber café's continues. He concludes that there are indeed Ghanaians and non-Ghanaians involved in cyber fraud and then discusses what repercussions this has to cyber café owners, the fraudsters, law enforcement agencies, and legislature.

## 239. Wisdome, J. Tettey

2008, 'Globalization, Cybersexuality Among Ghanaian Youth, and Moral Panic'. In Joselph Mensah (ed.), *Neoliberalism and Globalization in Africa: Contestations on the Embattled Continent*, New York: Palgrave Macmillan, pp. 157-176.

The author shows how globalization and the accompanying electronic medicated communication innovations have created a transnational Internet-related sex and sexuality that — when placed in a country with limited resources — has facilitated sexual consumption through racial, gendered, and national self-imaginations reproducing patterns of inequality within and beyond Ghana.

## 240. Van der Walt, Thomas and Marietha Nieman

2009, 'Vrouejeugboekskrywers oor die Ango-Boereoorlog: Realisme en Versoening na Decades van Avontuur en Nasionalisme', *Tydskrif vir Geesteswetenskappe*, Jg. 49, nr. 4, pp. 674-687.

This article discusses the changes (like the depiction of characters and conciliation) brought about by women writers. Using the Anglo-Boer War as a backdrop for this paper the author discusses while many children actively experienced the war they are not included in the books written by adults. Now the author looks at how children and youth books in the 1980s depict the war and how they differ from previous texts.

# Part IX

## Parenting and Children's Relations with Fathers

## 241. Hunter, Mark

2004, 'Fathers Without 'Amandla'?: Gender and Fatherhood Among IsiZulu Speakers', *The Journal of Natal and Zulu History*, Vol. 22, pp. 149-160.

The author sets out to investigate the gap between physical paternity and social paternity and the role of Zulu fathers. He points out that men's power in certain spheres, such as the abandonment of women they have impregnated, is linked to men's disempowerment in other spheres, notably economic. Men are enormously frustrated at being able to father children physically but unable to accept the social role being a father entails because of inability to pay 'inhlawulo', 'ilobolo' and acting as provider. This leads to 'ambiguous fatherhood', a situation in which manliness is partly boosted by being able to father children and yet men are deprived of the role associated with fatherhood.

## 242. Madhavan, Sangeetha, Nicholas W. Townsend, and Anita I. Garey

2008, "Absent Breadwinners': Father-Child Connections and Paternal Support in Rural South Africa', *Journal of Southern African Studies*, Vol. 34, no. 3, pp. 647-663.

The authors examine the association between children's connections to their fathers and paternal support. Using data on 272 children collected as part of a study of Children's Well-Being and Social Connections in the Agincourt sub-district of Mpumalanga, South Africa, they identify three types of connection between children and their fathers and four levels of paternal support. The authors present empirical evidence on histories of children's residence and support to advance three propositions: first, that children's co-residence with their fathers is neither an accurate nor a sufficient indicator that they are receiving paternal financial support; second, children are as likely to receive financial support from fathers who are not even members of the same household as from fathers with whom they are co-resident; and, finally, that children who receive support from their fathers for any part of their lives are likely to receive support consistently throughout their lives. These findings underscore the importance of using a more nuanced conceptualization and more inclusive measurement of father connection and support in order to determine the contributions that men make to their children.

### 243. Mulindwa, Innocent Najjumba and James P.M. Ntozi

2004, 'Mothers in the Informal Economy and Changes in Child Feeding and Caring Roles in Kampala, Uganda', *Africa Development*, Vol. 29, no. 3, pp. 114-130.

This article examines the child feeding and caring practices of mothers in an informal economy in Kampala City, Uganda, using qualitative data collected in 1996. It was found that the supplementary feeding of children in this context started as early as three weeks despite the widespread belief among mothers that full breastfeeding should go on up to at least three months. This action was justified in terms of insufficient milk, working away from home, maternal illness, increased appetite of the child, sex of the child, child illness and contraception. The article also shows that, due to financial constraints, working mothers rely heavily on relatives as childcare providers. The findings seem to contradict the popular belief that informal sector work is compatible with child rearing responsibilities.

### 244. Richter, Linda and Robert Morrell, (eds)

2006, *Baba: Men and Fatherhood in South Africa*, Cape Town: HSRC.

This volume grew out of the Fatherhood Project initiated in 2003 by the Child, Youth and Family Development Project at the Human Sciences Research Council of South Africa. The aim is to explore fatherhood more deeply, looking beyond the sheer biological aspect of being a father. The title 'Baba' has been chosen as this is the respectful term of address for any older male in South Africa and it encapsulates the ideals of the book. The book is divided into five sections: the major conceptual and theoretical themes; fatherhood in historical perspective; fathers and the media; being a father in contemporary South Africa; and local and international policies and programmes.

# Part X

## Research On/With Children and Youth

## 245. Abebe, Tatek

2009, 'Multiple Methods, Complex Dilemmas: Negotiating Socio-ethical Spaces in Participatory Research with Disadvantaged Children', *Children's Geographies*, Vol 7, Issue 4, pp. 451-465.

The author explores the methodological and socio-ethical dilemmas of researching with disadvantaged children in two contrasting fieldwork settings in Ethiopia discussing the challenges of adhering to dominant, 'Western' ethical principles and of creating and sharing ethical spaces during fieldwork. The author asserts that research ethics originating in the Global North entail standards that are difficult to apply in social, cultural and economic contexts elsewhere, and that these need to be reworked in reflexive ways during fieldwork. The indeterminate nature of grounded field research and the fluidity of its unfolding directions, make the contextualization of universal ethics in local ethos about childhood necessary as is the recognition of how fieldwork with children is a morally contested terrain embedded in and through personal, social and ethical spatiality.

## 246. Bell, Nancy

2008, 'Ethics in Child Research: Rights, Reason and Responsibilities', *Children's Geographies*, Vol. 6, No. 1, pp. 7-20

This paper explores the nature of the relationship between research ethics and children's rights by examining the historical origins of both concepts and then analysing several contemporary research ethics guidelines from a rights-based perspective. The analysis demonstrates that while many research ethics guidelines may contain references to human rights principles, implicit or otherwise, there is often a lack definition about what is meant by 'rights' and about the correlation between human rights principles and research ethics in practice. Within social sciences research, in particular, research ethics guidelines, including those guidelines specific to child research, noticeably lack direct reference to human rights principles such as those articulated within the UN Convention on the Rights of the Child (UNCRC). The paper argues that as child researchers do not stand apart from their obligations to protect and promote children's rights, research ethics guidelines relied upon by child researchers need to be informed by human rights principles and that those researchers may draw upon the UNCRC, in particular, to inform their consideration of inevitable ethical dilemmas arising within child research.

### 247. Chobokoane, Ntebaleng and Debbie Budlender

2002, 'Methodology used to measure Child-Care in the South African Time Use Survey', *Agenda: Feminist Media*, No. 51, pp. 73-89.

This paper focuses on the methodology adopted by Stats SA to measure child care, spontaneity in its reporting, and the implications for the measurement of unpaid labour. It explores the advantages of using Stas SA to measure child-care for better response to needs by individuals, community, and government. The paper concludes that the methodology used by Stats SA to prompt childcare had some success in picking up childcare, which would otherwise have been missed.

### 248. Clacherty, Glynis and David Donald

2007, 'Child Participation in Research: Reflections on Ethical Challenges in the Southern African Context', *African Journal of AIDS Research*, Vol. 6, no. 2, pp. 147-156.

The authors reflect on several challenges that particular cultural, socioeconomic and catastrophic factors (such as the HIV epidemic) pose to ethical practice in research involving child participation in a region such as southern Africa. With reference to concrete situations, they discuss research practices in relation to countering the widespread power disparity between adults and children; ensuring the authenticity of children's evidence; obtaining informed consent; ensuring non-malfeasance and beneficence; and preserving the anonymity of participants and their sources.

### 249. Francis, Dennis and Crispin Hemson

2009, 'Youth as Research Fieldworkers in a Context of HIV/AIDS', *African Journal of AIDS Research*, Vol. 8, no. 2, pp. 223-230.

This study addresses the advantages and challenges of using youth as researchers for youth issues through qualitative research in a context of HIV/AIDS. Drawing on observations of the process of training out-of-school youths as research fieldworkers in KwaZulu-Natal Province (South

Africa), reflecting on the interviews with respondents, and on focus group discussions with the young fieldworkers, the study found striking advantages to using fieldworkers who are close in their characteristics to that of respondents but also observed striking limitations. Specifically, the peer researchers struggled with the wish of some respondents to establish supportive friendships with them, they lacked the authority of an academic researcher, and they sometimes resorted to false promises in attempts to get cooperation.

## 250. Grover, Sonja

2004, 'Why Won't They Listen to Us? On Giving Power and Voice to Children Participating in Social Research', *Childhood. A Global Journal of Child Research,* Vol. 11, No. 1, pp. 81-93.

This article discusses the need for authentic social research with children given the fact that increasingly such research is being relied on to inform social policy which profoundly affects the lives of children. Authentic research is operationalized in this article as that research which gives power and voice to child research participants and which provides insights into their subjective world. Such research allows the children to a degree to be 'subject' or 'collaborator' in the research process rather than simply study 'object'. Giving power and voice to children in the research context involves issues of research methodology and opportunities to contribute to research agendas and ethics guidelines such that the need and right to be heard is better met. Empathetic understanding in research with children as a byproduct of combining quantitative approaches with the phenomenological perspective is also discussed.

## 251. Maundeni, Tapologo and Lisa Lopez Levers

2005, 'Concerns About Child Subject Research in Botswana: a Call for Establishing Structures and Guidelines that Protect Children', *African Sociological Review*, Vol. 9, no. 2, pp. 153-167.

This paper examines factors associated with child subject research and advances arguments that favour the articulation of explicit guidelines and protocols for research conducted with anyone under age. It offers a brief history of the ethics of human subject research and discusses the reality of contemporary research with children in Botswana against the backdrop of international ethical standards. Issues that need attention include how to avoid exposing children to stress; how to ensure that children's rights are protected; and how to ensure that scientifically qualified researchers are also adequately trained in relevant aspects of child development and related child concerns. The paper concludes with recommendations for policymaking at protecting the interests of children in Botswana.

## 252. Robson, Elsbeth, Porter, Gina, Hampshire, Kate and Bourdillon, Michael

2009, "Doing it Right?': Working with Young Researchers in Malawi to Investigate Children, Transport and Mobility', *Children's Geographies*, Vol 7, Issue 4, pp. 467-480.

This paper explores involving children in Malawi in research about young people, mobility and transport, respecting their rights of participation, education, and protection from exploitation. The Malawi study forms one component of a research project taking place in three sub-Saharan African countries. A foundation of the larger project was the conviction that children are experts on their own lives; therefore seeking children's views was essential, thus respecting the UNCRC. We also embraced an ethical approach, that 'the best interests of the child shall be a primary consideration'. We reflect on challenges in putting ethical principles into practice in the inevitably messy real world.

## 253. Shung King, M., September, R., Okatcha, F.M. and Cardoso, C., (eds)

2009, *Child Research In Africa, The African Child Research Network Initiative Report on the colloquium held on 21 and 22 November 2006, Dakar, Senegal*, Council for the Development of Social Science Research in Africa (CODESRIA) and Childwatch International. CODESRIA, Dakar.

This a monograph undertaken by Childwatch International and CODESRIA in collaboration with the Child and Youth Research and Training Programme at the University of Western Cape, South Africa, the Children's Institute at the University of Cape Town and Kenyatta University in Nairobi, Kenya. It comprises three papers that were presented at that occasion as well as the discussion that follows. Recognising the challenges that face researchers and their institutions, and the existing gap between policy makers and researchers, the monograph is an excellent evaluation of the child research potential in Africa. It examines the feasibility of the child research on the continent by exploring ways through which researchers and institutions across Africa can strengthen the quantity and the quality of child research in Africa. An assessment of the available research resources, in particular the technical skills of African researchers, and available financial resources is also part of the analyses.

## 254. Young, Lorraine and Barrett, Hazel

2001, 'Issues of Access and Identity Adapting Research Methods with Kampala Street Children', *Childhood. A Global Journal of Child Research,* Vol. 8, No. 3, pp. 383-395.

The issues of researcher access and identity are important ethical considerations when researching children. They are particularly significant when the children are a highly marginalized group such as those living on the street. Using research with street children in Kampala, Uganda, as an exemplar, this article explores the methodological issues associated with gaining access to street children and reducing the influence of the researcher's 'outsider' identity, when undertaking sociospatial research. Through the adoption of a child-centred methodology and the adaptation of ethnographic, oral and visual methods, in conjunction with the children themselves, this article illustrates how meaningful results can be gleaned without the inhibitory effects of limited access and outsider influence.

# Part XI

## Rituals, Beliefs, and Spirituality

## 255. Amenga-Etego, Rose Mary

2008, 'Chinchirisi: the phenomenon of 'spirit children' among the Nankani of northern Ghana', *Legon Journal of the Humanities*, Vol. 19, pp. 183-214.

In this paper author discusses the identity of the 'spirit child' (chinchirigo) that is often ambiguous, but still remains a vital component of the religio-cultural system of the Nankani of northern Ghana. Like other belief systems in Africa, the chinchirisi phenomenon is not limited to people's spirituality. It transcends the realm of the sacred into the daily lives of the community as a form of explanation of the puzzles and complexities of life. The article examines how some of the practices associated with the phenomenon are becoming a source of concern in contemporary society. In particular, it explores in what ways and to what extent this religiocultural phenomenon is a challenge to euthanasia, human rights and rural development in contemporary society.

## 256. Berliner, David

2005, 'An "Impossible" Transmission: Youth Religious Memories in Guinea–Conakry', *American Ethnologist*, Volume 32. Issue 4, pp. 576 – 592.

This paper contributes to an increasing anthropological interest in youth agency by inviting readers to look at youth as a crucial site for understanding issues of religious memory and cultural transmission. The author shows that in the past five decades, Bulongic people (Guinea–Conakry) have undergone significant religious changes caused by the introduction of Islam, which has led to the official disappearance of pre-Islamic rituals. The article explores how young Bulongic remember a pre-Islamic past that they have never experienced, and argues that, to understand how they assimilate and perpetuate this religious heritage, one must examine the subtle processes of intergenerational transmission through which their memories are dynamically shaped.

## 257. Gottlieb, Alma

2005, 'Babies' Baths, Babies' Remembrances: a Beng Theory of Development, History and Memory', *Africa: Journal of the International African Institute*, Vol. 75, no. 1, pp. 105-118.

In this essay, which is necessarily to some extent speculative given its subject of infant memory, the author explores the allegorical implications of the Beng afterlife, suggesting that the attribution of heightened infant memory of an idyllic 'wrugbe' serves as an indirect critique of French colonialism and its aftermath. She concludes by discussing the ways in which memory and forgetting are mutually constructed, with the Beng model offering substantial support for the contention that reproduction in general - and babies in particular - are crucial to this intertwined process.

## 258. Munthali, Alister C.

2002, 'After Delivery: Attempts to Protect Children from 'Tsempho' in A Rural Malawian Village', *Society of Malawi Journal*. Vol. 55, no. 1, pp. 24-37.

Based on fieldwork conducted in 1999 in the area of TA Malemia, Zomba district, Malawi, the author describes the different ritual processes that take place after the birth of a child and before its parents can resume sexual intercourse. These include the seclusion of a newly born baby after birth; the administration of 'likambako', the medicines and other rituals which protect newly born babies against illnesses believed to be caused by sexual intercourse; and the declaration of adultery by men.

## 259. Obadare, Ebenezer

2007, 'White-Collar Fundamentalism: Interrogating Youth Religiosity on Nigerian University Campuses', *The Journal of Modern African Studies*, Vol. 45, no. 4, pp. 517-537.

This paper aims to locate youthful angst displayed by Nigerian university students within the context of postcolonial anomie and the attendant immiseration of civil society. Youth religious extremism on Nigerian campuses reflects both young people's frustration with national processes, and their perceived alienation from modernity's 'cosmopolitan conversation'. The author tries to understand the intersection between global economic forces and increased religiosity among campus youth in Nigerian universities.

## 260. Van Beek, Walter E.A.

2002, 'Why a Twin is not a Child: Symbols in Kapsiki Birth Rituals', *Journal des africanistes*, Vol. 72, no. 1, pp. 119-147.

This article examines the position of twins among the Kapsiki of Cameroon and Nigeria through a comparison of the differences in cultural constructs of a 'normal' (single) birth and a twin birth, and through an analysis of the symbols and rituals surrounding the various types of birth. It appears that among the Kapsiki birth rites for ´normal´ births gradually incorporate the infant into the kin group, protecting the mother and the child against evil influences. Twin birth rites are quite different. Other symbolic objects and a specific discourse are used. Twins form a special society within Kapsigi villages, due to the danger they are believed to pose for their parents. The symbolic position of twins is related to male initiation. The author concludes that twins are symbolically positioned on the fringe of Kapsiki society.

# Part XII

## Street Children, Ex-combatants, and Rehabilitation

## 261. Abbink, Jon and Ineke van Kessel, (ed.)

2005, *Vanguard or Vandals: Youth, Politics and Conflict in Africa,* Leiden; Boston: Brill.

This volume contains a range of original studies on the controversial role of youth in politics, conflicts and rebellious movements in Africa. A common aim of the studies is to try and explain why patterns of generational conflict and violent response among younger age groups in Africa are showing such a remarkably uneven spread across the continent.

## 262. Abdullah, Ibrahim

2002, 'Youth Culture and Rebellion: Understanding Sierra Leone's Wasted Decade', *Critical Arts,* Vol. 16, no. 2, pp. 19-37.

This paper deals with the centrality of rebellious youth culture in understanding Sierra Leone's wasted decade, 1991-2000. It argues that the socially constructed borders marking the different categories of youth began to shift in the late 1960s and 1970s under the strains of political repression and the emergence of an ' imagined community' constructed around the 'odelay' (carnival) societies and the neighbourhood. The result was a kind of fusion between the mainstream and 'rarray' (unacceptable) youth cultures, which inaugurated a political conversation anchored on the use of violence. The central argument of the paper revolves around the role of subaltern culture in the making of an alternative political route to power in postcolonial Africa.

## 263. Adebanwi, Wale

2005, 'The Carpenter's Revolt: Youth, Violence and the Reinvention of Culture in Nigeria', *The Journal of Modern African Studies,* Vol. 43, no. 3, pp. 339-365.

This paper draws on Bourdieu's notion of habitus and Gramsci's 'agential' conception of culture to explore the construction and activities of the OPC. In particular, it examines the cultural repertoires of the youthful, 'militant' faction of the OPC, pointing to ways in which violence and ritual can be interpreted both as an instrumentally rational strategy of power struggle and as a form of symbolic action with cultural meanings. The OPC case strongly challenges the bifurcation of tradition and modernity, given the way the group appropriates culture in negotiating Yoruba identity, while also retaining democratic rhetoric. The paper argues that the activities of the OPC constitute not stable, bounded manifestations of culture, but rather fluid, ambivalent and paradoxical ethnic-power relations and formations.

### 264. Arowosegbe, Jeremiah O.

2009, 'Violence and National Development in Nigeria: the Political Economy of Youth Restiveness in the Niger Delta', *Review of African Political Economy*, Vol. 36, no. 122, pp. 575-594.

This article examines the factors that influence youth restiveness in Nigeria's Niger Delta region. It discusses the impact of conservative elite politics and the oil-centric political economy characterized by the impoverishment, neglect and repression of the oil-producing communities on the youth in the region. The article raises questions about the violence-development dialectic, drawing upon the context, dynamics, explanations and impact of youth violence in Nigeria's oil-rich Niger Delta. It examines the contradictions and injustices existing against the ethnic minorities of the oil-bearing communities in the region resulting from the centralization of oil revenues by the federal centre and how these have generated marginalization and violent conflict.

### 265. Atieno, Awinda

2007, 'Mungiki, 'Neo-Mau Mau' & the Prospects for Democracy in Kenya', *Review of African Political Economy*, Vol. 34, no. 113, pp. 526-531.

This paper deals with the Mungiki, an armed vigilante gang of destitute youths in Kenya, which began as a spiritual movement in the early 1990s in the Rift Valley. In the middle of the 1990s, Mungiki had moved to the Nairobi slums, and had become a dynamic player in the most important market in Nairobi's lawless areas: violence. Mungiki could be the new Mau Mau. The author examines this gang, based on fieldwork carried out amongst youth activists in Nairobi from 2004 to 2007, amongst others presenting fragments of the Sheng hip-hop poetry used by these youths to describe and come up with solutions to their desperate situation as the lowest economic class in Nairobi.

## 266. Baines, Erin K.

2009, 'Complex Political Perpetrators: Reflections on Dominic Ongwen', *The Journal of Modern African Studies*, Vol. 47, no. 2, pp. 163-191.

The author introduces the concept of complex political perpetrators to describe youth who occupy extremely marginal spaces in settings of chronic crisis, and who use violence as an expression of political agency. This paper focuses on Dominic Ongwen, an indicted war criminal and former child soldier in one of the world's most brutal rebel organizations, the Lord's Resistance Army (LRA) in Uganda. Ongwen is at once victim and perpetrator: what justice strategy is relevant? Ongwen represents a troupe of young rebels who were 'bred' in the shadows of illiberal war economies. The author argues that you like Ongwen are often excluded from the polity, or rather never get socialized within it, forming complex political identities that must be recognized in the debate on transitional justice after mass atrocity, lest cycles of exclusion and violence as politics by another means continue.

## 267. Bank, Leslie

2003, 'Comrades, Cats and Country Boys: Youth Style, City Streets and the Politics of Home in East London's Townships, 1950-1998', *Anthropology Southern Africa*, Vol. 26, no. 1/2, pp. 29-41.

This article focuses on the changing identity politics and social position of youth in the townships of East London in the Eastern Cape of South Africa between the 1950s and the 1990s. It is centrally concerned with the fluid and changing relationships between different categories of youth in the city's locations over time. Three categories of youth receive particular attention: the 'oobrighty' or fashion conscious urban youth (also known as the Cats); the comrades or 'amaqabane', the political youth of the 1980s and 1990s; and the rural youth that flowed into the city from surrounding homelands. Arguing that the critical role of rural youth in urban transformation is often underplayed, the author shows that one of the reasons why the comrades in East London were able to consolidate power with such force in the 1980s was because they were able to breakdown older barriers. He also shows that the convergence of urban and rural youth identities and styles was reflected in the reconstruction of youth domesticity, especially with the large-scale adoption of 'ukuhlalisana' (living together outside marriage) as the preferred domestic style amongst both urban and rural youth in the 1980s.

## 268. Bay, Edna G. and Donald L. Donham

2006, *States of Violence: Politics, Youth, and Memory in Contemporary Africa*. Charlottesville, VA: University of Virginia Press.

Exploring violence as part of political economy and rejecting stereotypical explanations of African violence as endemic or natural to African cultures, the essays in this volume examine a continent where the boundaries on acceptable force are always shifting and the distinction between violence by the State and against the State is not always clear. Many of the essays address generational tensions through the role of African youth, who in this context are almost exclusively male. Other essays examine the temptation in an atmosphere of violence to exploit the malleability of memory to (re)construct histories in order to justify the sacrifices brought by that violence.

## 269. Bøås, Morten and Anne Hatløy

2008, "Getting in, Getting Out': Militia Membership and Prospects for Re-integration in Post-War Liberia', *The Journal of Modern African Studies*, Vol. 46, no. 1, pp. 33-55.

The data that form the basis of this article suggest a picture different from that painted about Liberian ex-combatants that are generally seen as uprooted urban youths with a history of unemployment, underemployment and idleness. After interviewing 491 ex-combatants in Monrovia, the authors argue that what caused the Liberian youth to fight were mainly security concerns, suggesting that the effects of 'idleness' and 'unemployment' are overstated with regards to people joining armed groups. The ex-combatants went to school, worked and lived with parents or close relatives prior to the war, meaning that they are not T. Mkandawire's (2002) uprooted urban youths or I. Abdullah's (1998) 'lumpens'. They lived quite ordinary Liberian lives, and based their decision on whether to join an armed group on the security predicament that they believed that they and their families were facing. This suggests that disarmament, demobilization, reintegration and rehabilitation approaches are in need of re-thinking that links them more directly to social cohesion and societal security.

## 270. Brennan, James R.

2006, 'Youth, the TANU Youth League and Managed Vigilantism in Dar es Salaam, Tanzania, 1925-73', *Africa: International African Institute*, Vol. 76, no. 2, pp. 221-246.

This article examines the role of male youth in the political history of Dar es Salaam (Tanzania). 'Youth', as a category of opposition to elders, became important during the interwar period as it was inhabited by educated African bureaucrats aspiring to representation in urban politics over the traditional claims of authority by local ethnic Zaramo and Shomvi elders. The author discusses how repeated reassertion of party control over its Youth League took many forms in the decade after independence - through the creation of a National Service; frequent nationalist events and rituals where Youth League members controlled public space; and a war on urban morality led by Youth League shock troops. Control over youth also offered a potentially autonomous patrimony for ambitious TANU party members. The 1970s witnessed the beginning of the general failure of both State and party to generate sufficient resources to serve as a patron to patron-seeking youth, which has effectively decentralized youth violence and vigilantism ever since.

## 271. Burton, Andrew

2006, 'Raw Youth, School-Leavers and the Emergence of Structural Unemployment in Late-Colonial Urban Tanganyika', *The Journal of African History*, Vol. 47, no. 3, p. 363-387.

This article examines the historical origins of one of urban Africa's most visible contemporary problems, using Tanzania as a case study. The middle decades of the twentieth century are identified as a time when a pivotal shift occurred as labour scarcity gave way to oversupply, resulting in the emergence of enduring 'structural' unemployment. The latter part of the article describes the panicked response of the incoming African regime, faced with what they initially interpreted as a potentially insurrectionary class of urban unemployed. Closing remarks speculate on whether, in the longue durée, one may interpret unemployment in a more positive light as part of an ongoing wider historical transformation.

## 272. Christensen, Maya M. and Mats Utas

2008, 'Mercenaries of Democracy: the 'Politricks' of Remobilized Combatants in the 2007 General Elections, Sierra Leone', *African Affairs*, Vol. 107, no. 429, pp. 515-539.

In this article the authors show how political parties strategically remobilized ex-combatants into 'security squads' in order both to protect themselves and to mobilize votes. They look at the tactical and strategic motives behind ex-combatants' choice to join the political campaigning and the alternatives (such as 'watermelon politics'), and they also examine the deep distrust between politicians and ex-combatants. Focusing on politics as the domestication of violence, they shed light on the continuation of pre-war and war-time mobilization of youth into politics and demonstrate how electoral moments can legitimize violence. In hindsight, the 2007 elections strengthened the democratic process in Sierra Leone, but this article shows on what fragile ground this success was built.

## 273. Davies, Matthew

2008, 'A Childish Culture? Shared Understandings, Agency and Intervention: an Anthropological Study of Street children in Northwest Kenya', *Childhood. A Global Journal of Child Research*, Vol. 15, No. 3, p. 309-330

This article shows how group solidarity is maintained through the sharing of a common subculture of spatial understandings, games, activities, dress, language and bodily actions. Street children in Makutano, northwest Kenya, form strong, stable social groups and group activity functions through a well-defined structure involving leadership and close personal and economic relationships. Through the group, the children experience a quality of life that negates the validity of common interventionist strategies used by many organizations or government arms. The author concludes that given their high levels of competency, policies for working with these street children should be based on dialogue and should act to empower them through expanding the choices available to them.

## 274. De Boeck, Filip

2006, 'Youth, Death and the Urban Imagination: a Case from Kinshasa', *Bulletin des séances: Académie royale des sciences d'outre-mer*, Année 52, no. 2, pp. 113-125.

This article reflects on mourning rituals as they emerge today among young urbanites in Kinshasa. The changing practices surrounding the place of death in the city are analysed as specific ways in which young Kinois urbanites not only contest the realm of official politics and dominant religious discourses and practices, but also use the instance of death to rethink and reposition themselves in the light of a broader, essentially moral, crisis. Paradoxically, urban youth seem to revive more 'traditional' forms of 'rituals of rebellion' and tap into moral matrixes with much older roots, thereby inventing a future for traditions that are themselves already reinvented in the urban context. The article is based on several years of field research in Kinshasa, most recently in September 2005.

## 275. De Wet, Corene

2006, 'Bullebakkery: Almal se Probleem', *Tydskrif vir Geesteswetenskappe*, Jg. 46, nr. 1, pp. 87-100.

This study reports on an investigation into aspects of bullying in schools in the Free State, South Africa. It appears that there are few Free State learners who have never been exposed, either as victims and/or as witnesses, to direct and/or indirect verbal bullying. Furthermore, it seems that the victims of bullies prefer to take fellow learners rather than adults into their confidence if they are being victimized. Victims are also more likely to be assisted by fellow learners than by adults. Learners who are willing to help fellow learners prefer to help in cases of verbal rather than physical bullying. The article concludes that educators, parents and learners should accept equal responsibility for the battle against bullying.

## 276.  Doom, Ruddy and Koen Vlassenroot

2001, 'Violent Culture or a Culture of Violence?: Militia-Formation in Eastern Congo', in *Politics and Economics of Africa*, ed. Frank Columbus, Huntington, N.Y.: Nova Science Publishers.Vol. 1: pp. 57-81.

The authors outline the historical background of the dynamics of cultural change and conflict in eastern Congo and deal with the ongoing Mayi-Mayi rebellion in this area. When it comes to sub-Saharan Africa, conflicts are mostly interpreted in cultural terms. As opposed to this, the authors argue that, with the formation of grassroots militias, rural and urban youth resist the effects of State implosion and the different foreign armed interventions and motivate their actions on an ethnic ideology. In doing so, they combine former traditions of resistance and violence with newly developed patterns of mobility in an interpretation of customary defence that is based on the social meaning of land.

## 277.  Droz, Yvan

2006, 'Street Children and the Work Ethic New Policy for an Old Moral, Nairobi (Kenya)', *Childhood. A Global Journal of Child Research,* Vol. 13, No. 3, pp. 349-363.

This paper explores a number of issues related to power, safety, and livelihood connected to street children. The author argues that Kenyan policy-makers use the language of children's rights to legitimize, within the new global political order, an old colonial concern about controlling the urban marginal population. The local business community's worries about the safety of Nairobi's streets stand paramount, while the growing financial and political leverage of NGOs interfering in local affairs in the name of street children's rights is looked upon with suspicion. Accusing the abstract universalism of the language of children's rights of being incompatible with local values, the local political elite seeks to muster support by offering an alternative version based on the local Kikuyu ethos of the 'accomplished man'. This version sits well with international development agencies' abandonment of the term 'street children' in favour of 'street families'. Deportation and forced labour of children and youth are sanctified as moral imperatives expected to restore the meaning of family to its rightful place in the local business morale.

## 278. Evans, Ruth M.C.

2004, 'Tanzanian Childhoods: Street Children's Narratives of 'Home'', *Journal of Contemporary African Studies*. Vol. 22, no. 1, pp. 69-92.

Using empirical data from ethnographic, child-focused research with street children in Tanzania, the author discusses children's narratives of their home environments. She attempts a holistic analysis of the experiences of family life and their home environment, which have influenced their decisions to leave home for the street. Poverty and household instability, corporal punishment, the conflict between ' work' and 'play', underlying gender inequalities, children's experiences within diverse household structures, and rural-urban migration are identified as salient motivating factors.

## 279. Fair, Jo Ellen

2008/09, 'Crafting Lifestyles in Urban Africa: Young Ghanaians in the World of Online Friendship', *Africa Today*, Vol. 55, no. 4, pp. 29-49.

Through in-depth interviews and observations, the authors consider one aspect of Internet practice in Africa: how use of the Internet for making friends and dating allows young, urban Ghanaians to craft lifestyles, incorporating globally circulating cultural and symbolic forms into their identities. They suggest that when young, urban Ghanaians go online to meet, chat, and form relationships with strangers near and far, they are devising, testing out, and sharing sensibilities; they are bringing situation, mood, and new knowledge to bear on the self or selves that they are exploring and tentatively projecting. The study is based on observations in six Internet cafés in four distinct, economically diverse neighbourhoods in Accra, Ghana, in January 2008.

## 280. Fegley, Randall

2008/09, 'Comparative Perspectives on the Rehabilitation of Ex-Slaves and Former Child Soldiers with Special Reference to Sudan', *African Studies Quarterly*, Vol. 10, no. 1, pp. 35-69.

This article tabulates the successes and failures of governmental and non-governmental programmes rehabilitating former slaves, many of whom were or are children, and child soldiers, many of whom are now adults. It compares activities in Sudan to programmes in other parts of Africa (Angola, Ethiopia, Ghana, Liberia, Mozambique, Sierra Leone and Uganda) and beyond (Afghanistan, India, Sri Lanka and the United Arab Emirates). Applying these comparisons in the absence of long-term assessments, the author endeavours to determine pitfalls to be avoided and best practices to be followed.

## 281. Francis, David J.

2007, 'Paper Protection' Mechanisms: Child Soldiers and the International Protection of Children in Africa's Conflict Zones', *The Journal of Modern African Studies*, Vol. 45, no. 2, pp. 207-231.

This paper is based on extensive fieldwork carried out in Liberia and Sierra Leone over three years (2001-2003) that reveals that the application of the restrictive and Western-centric definition and construction of a 'child' and 'childhood' raises inherent difficulties in the African context. Further, the author argues that most war-torn and post-conflict African societies are faced with the challenge of incorporating international customary laws into their domestic laws. The failure of the international community to enforce its standards on child soldiers also has to do with the politics of ratification of international treaties, in particular the fear by African governments of setting dangerous precedents, since they are also culpable of recruitment and use of child soldiers.

## 282. Geenen, Kristien

2009, "Sleep Occupies no Space': the Use of Public Space by Street Gangs in Kinshasa', *Africa: International African Institute*, Vol. 79, no. 3, pp. 347-368.

This article deals with issues of territoriality, public space, the microphysics of power and street gang life in the current urban context of Kinshasa, capital of the Democratic Republic of Congo. In this city, a growing number of street children invade the public places. They team up in gangs and scour the streets in search of a location to settle (for a while). This contribution considers this dynamic field of negotiations through a focus on space and analyses it from a Foucauldian angle. It explores how gang members develop particular ways to control their territories and exercise power in them. Additionally, it examines how street youths manage to construct a home in the streets and make sense of their urban environment in the process.

## 283. Ginsburg, Carren

2009, 'Patterns of Residential Mobility Amongst Children in Greater Johannesburg-Soweto, South Africa: Observations from the Birth to Twenty Cohort', *Urban Forum*, Vol. 20, no. 4, pp. 397-413.

This paper presents results from a 14-year longitudinal study of child residential movement in the Greater Johannesburg area, using data collected through the Birth to Twenty Research Programme (BT20). The paper analyses the frequencies and patterns of residential mobility observed over the first 14 years of the lives of children in BT20 cohort. Of the 3,273 children enrolled in the cohort in 1990, two thirds of the children have moved home at least once. Nonetheless, a third of the children have never moved, indicating some stability among the urban child population. Residential moves by children were found to be associated with both the lowest resourced and the highest resourced households.

## 284. Gomez-Perez, Muriel, Marie-Nathalie LeBlanc, and Mathias Savadogo

2009, 'Young Men and Islam in the 1990s: Rethinking an Intergenerational Perspective', *Journal of Religion in Africa*, Vol. 39, no. 2, pp. 186-218.

This paper examines the sociopolitical role of young men in Islamic revivalist movements that occurred in urban centres in Côte d'Ivoire, Burkina Faso and Senegal in the 1980-1990s. Such movements were particularly popular among secularly educated young men who attended French-speaking schools. While the role of young men in revivalist movements suggests new configurations of authority and charisma, their religious agency remains closely embedded within relationships that extend across generations. The paper looks at instances of conflicts between generations and pays attention to sites of negotiation, such as mosques and voluntary associations.

## 285.  Grant, Miriam

2003, 'Difficult Debut: Social and Economic Identities of Urban Youth in Bulawayo, Zimbabwe', *Canadian Journal of African Studies*, Vol. 37, no. 2/3, pp. 411-439.

This article examines social and economic identities of urban youth in Zimbabwe on the basis of interviews conducted in 1998 and 1999 in three high density suburbs - Nkulumane, Luveve, Lobengula - in Bulawayo, the second largest city of Zimbabwe. The data presented derive from 120 household dyad interviews with youth and their parents and guardians. The article aims to tease out some of the linkages between education and skill levels, economic and housing vulnerability, and social relations for youth in the urban arena. It also explores how youth are taking responsibility for their social and economic identities and how household members and, to a lesser extent, the community plays a role in this process. In this context, the article finishes with a brief exploration of the idea of the development and nurturance of youth as a significant aspect of social capital.

## 286.  Grant, Miriam

2006, "I have been Patient Enough': Gendered Futures and Mentors of Female Youth in Urban Zimbabwe', *Social Dynamics*, Vol. 32, no. 1, pp. 21-46.

This article examines the gendered futures of female youth and how mentors impact their journey towards adulthood. It is based on longitudinal research involving household dyad interviews with youth/ young adults and parents or guardians in high density suburbs of Bulawayo, Zimbabwe, between 1998 and 2001. The article sets the context of severe economic collapse and the raging AIDS epidemic in Zimbabwe.

## 287.  Groes-Green, Christian

2009, 'Hegemonic and Subordinated Masculinities: Class, Violence and Sexual Performance Among Young Mozambican Men', *Nordic Journal of African Studies*, Vol. 18, no. 4, pp. 286-304.

This article explores theoretical implications of sexual and violent practices among disenfranchised young men in Mozambique. Findings from research carried out in Maputo in 2007, 2008 and 2010 indicate that massive unemployment caused by neoliberal reforms has led to a growing number of young men basing their authority vis-à-vis women on bodily power, understood as the abilities and physique of the male body, rather than on economic power and social status. While young men from the city's growing middle class enact hegemonic masculinities in relationships with female partners by means of financial power and adherence to a 'breadwinner's' ideology, young men who are poor react to a situation of unemployment and poverty by enacting masculinities that are subordinate vis-à-vis middle-class peers, but which find expression through violence or sexual performance visà-vis female partners. The article is based on fieldwork consisting of a survey involving 500 young men and women, 8 focus group discussions with 90 informants between 16 and 23 years of age and in-depth interviews. Of the 90 informants, 21 were middle-class youth from the urban city centre and 69 were youth from working class backgrounds in impoverished suburban areas.

## 288. Ifeka, Caroline

2006, 'Youth Cultures and the Fetishization of Violence in Nigeria', *Review of African Political Economy*, Vol. 33, no. 110, pp. 721-736.
The author develops a conceptual framework for analysing youth cultures of resistance and violence in the context of customary and world religions in which old and new gods are important sources of ideological resistance. Condensing around points of intersection between capital and non-capitalist kin-based economies in Nigeria's oil-producing Niger Delta, she argues that militant youth cultures develop through a 'double' articulation between 'parent' cultures largely producing use values, and capitalist cultures pervaded by world religions (Christianity, Islam).

## 289. Keen, David

2003, 'Greedy Elites, Dwindling Resources, Alienated Youths: the Anatomy of Protracted Violence in Sierra Leone', *Internationale Politik und Gesellschaft*, H. 2, pp. 67-94.
This paper argues that state collapse and civil war in Sierra Leone cannot be adequately understood in terms of the political economy of diamond mining, but rather, in the lack of economic progress as well as bad

governance, that in turn generate a frustrated generation of youths no longer controlled by traditional social ties and available for organized violence. The author further argues that current 'reconstruction' is reinventing several phenomena that fed into the conflict. These include neoliberalism, continuing debt repayments, a neglect of industry, endemic corruption, the chieftaincy system, a dysfunctional legal system, and a focus of civil society activity and international assistance on Freetown.

### 290. Konings, Piet

2006, 'Bendskin Drivers in Douala's New Bell Neighbourhood: Masters of the Road and the City', in *Crisis and creativity: exploring the wealth of the African neighbourhood*, ed. Piet Konings and Dick Foeken, Leiden: Brill, pp. 46-65.

The youth of New Bell, one of the largest and poorest immigrant quarters in Douala, Cameroon, have invented a new activity: using motorbikes as taxis. This is commonly known as 'bendskin', an activity that is not only securing them a sustainable livelihood during the current economic crisis and structural adjustment, but also is making a significant contribution to solving the neighbourhood's critical transport problem. Bendskin drivers are usually organized in small groups along ethnic and friendship lines, and form a social and spatial 'neighbourhood' within the New Bell neighbourhood as a whole. Nevertheless, they have also proved themselves capable of transcending group boundaries and rally round when one of their colleagues or their common interests are threatened by outsiders, such as other road users and, more particularly, the police. Due to their sheer number and ability to mobilize so rapidly, they constitute a powerful force, which has made them the 'masters of the road', and, on certain occasions, even the 'masters of the city'.

### 291. Konings, Piet

2006/07, 'Solving Transportation Problems in African Cities: Innovative Responses by the Youth in Douala, Cameroon', *Africa Today*. Vol. 53, no. 1, pp. 35-50.

This study focuses on responses by young people in Cameroon, showing how the youth of New Bell, one of the largest and poorest immigrant quarters in Douala, have devised two innovative activities: one, commonly known as 'bendskin', is the use of motorbikes as taxis; the other, 'pousse-pousse', is the use of handcarts for transporting merchandise. These activities not only secure a sustainable livelihood and a feeling of self-esteem, but also make a contribution to solving the neighbourhood's transportation problems. The paper also shows that bendskin drivers and pousseurs (handcart operators) are usually organized in small groups along ethnic and friendship lines, and form a social and spatial 'neighborhood' within New Bell.

## 292. Leonardi, Cherry

2007, "'Liberation' or Capture: Youth in Between 'Hakuma' and 'Home' During Civil War and its Aftermath in Southern Sudan', *African Affairs*, Vol. 106, no. 424, pp. 391-412.

This article examines a structural opposition in Southern Sudan between the sphere of military/government (the 'hakuma') and the sphere of 'home'. It argues that to be a 'youth' in Southern Sudan means to inhabit the tensions of the space between these spheres. While attempting to resist capture by either sphere, youth have used their recruitment by the military to invest in their home or family sphere. Their aspiration to 'responsibility' illustrates not generational rebellion, but the moral continuity in local society, also evident in discussions of marriage.

## 293. Maina, Grace

2009, 'Human Securitised Reintegration of Formerly Abducted Children in Northern Uganda', *African Security Review*, Vol. 18, no. 4, pp. 115-122.

This paper focuses on the reintegration component of demobilisation and reintegration (DDR) with regard to child combatants in Uganda and analyses the process of reintegration, the gaps in the current reintegration literature and practice, the challenges of the process, and the role played by the various actors in northern Uganda that enable formerly abducted children to gain a civilian lifestyle.

## 294. Mamman, M.

2004, 'Urban Youth Violence as a Threat to Urban Security and Governance in Nigeria', *Savanna*, Vol. 19, no. 1, pp. 87-101.

This paper addresses some of the causal factors of urban youth violence and ethnoreligious conflicts in four urban centres -Aba, Kaduna, Kano and Lagos - in Nigeria. The main thrust of the paper is how violence threatens Nigeria's nascent democracy, as well as the corporate existence of the country. The paper is based on a survey using 1200 questionnaires carried out between 1 December 2000 and 31 January 2001. It concludes that poverty, political and social exclusion and marginalization, as well as economic deprivation are all working against the solidarity that would enable city inhabitants to live together despite their differences.

## 295. Margaretten, Emily

2011, 'Standing (K) in: Street Youth and Street Relatedness in South Africa', *City & Society*, Volume 23. Issue 1, pp. 45 – 65.

This paper examines the social attachments of youth living on the streets of Durban, South Africa. The author investigates their interactions with one another as friends, kin, and conjugal lovers, and as such, draws attention to the variability and creativity of youth fellowships in the city. This study argues that there are critical linkages of belonging on the streets that are framed by institutional forces yet also by the interpersonal subjectivities of youth who imaginatively negotiate their relatedness to one another and in the process, their standing in South African society.

## 296. Mathabatha, Sello

2004, 'The 1976 Student Revolts and the Schools in Lebowa, 1970-1976', *South African Historical Journal*, No. 51, pp. 108-129.

Focusing on missionary, former missionary and specialized schools within the homeland of Lebowa and drawing mostly from interviews, this paper shows that the Soweto uprisings also had an impact on some Lebowa schools, especially schools in which Afrikaans was introduced as the medium of instruction, because of the inconsistency in the Lebowa government's implementation of language policy. The paper also acknowledges the fact that the lack of a common youth culture in many community schools in the homeland served to limit the impact of the 1976 student uprising on Lebowa. Furthermore, the continual changes of youth culture in the homeland fostered the development of a youth consciousness necessary for political mobilization. Tertiary institutions such as the University of the North also played a crucial role as a political catalyst in the region.

## 297. McCaskie, T.C

2008, 'Gun Culture in Kumasi', *Africa: Journal of the International African Institute*, Vol. 78, no. 3, pp. 433-454.

This article is about gun culture in Kumasi, historic capital of Asante and Ghana's second city. Gun use in Asante, and elsewhere in Ghana, has increased significantly in the last decade. In practice and in the public imagination this is associated with the rise of youth gangs and the criminalization of urban space. Much has been written about youths and violence elsewhere in Africa, but this article focuses on the neglected topic of guns themselves - their manufacture, sale, distribution, use and meanings. It is the purpose of this article to add to the growing literature on 'violent youth' in Africa, but to do so from the viewpoint of the weapons that enable this violence.

## 298. McIntyre, Angela and Thokozani Thusi

2003, 'Children and Youth in Sierra Leone's Peace-Building Process', *African Security Review*, Vol. 12, no. 2, pp. 73-80.

This article, which is based on field trips to Sierra Leone in 2002, focuses on the politicization and abuse of children and youth in the Sierra Leone conflict and the resulting marginalization of these two groups since the cessation of hostilities. It argues that the country's experience demonstrates that children and youth are used (both as perpetrators and victims) as 'political currency' in conflicts and are not adequately protected by international law. The youth of Sierra Leone need to be given more political space (as they occupied during the war) to articulate their needs and be provided with enough opportunities to make them responsible citizens.

## 299. McIntyre, Angela

2003, 'Rights, Root Causes and Recruitment: the Youth Factor in Africa's Armed Conflicts', *African security Review*, Vol. 12, no. 2, pp. 91-99.

This article explores the ways in which African youth are mobilized to support political and military agendas. It suggests that a clearer understanding of these dynamics is necessary if peace-building interventions and postconflict recovery efforts are to be sustainable. The militarization of disaffected young people, of which the problem of child soldiers is only a small part, originates with the idea that youth constitute 'potential': a commodity that can and has been plundered alongside natural resources and public funds to serve the agendas of warfare.

## 300. McIntyre, Angela, (ed.)

2005, *Invisible Stakeholders: Children and War in Africa*, Pretoria: Institute for Security Studies.

This collective volume uses case studies from Angola, Sierra Leone, Ethiopia, Mozambique and Uganda to illustrate the roles of children and youth in war and change in Africa, from the child soldier to the youth activist, and suggests that the 'youth factor' is an important dimension of security analysis.

## 301. Morelle, Marie

2006, 'Les Enfants des Rues, l'État et les ONG: qui Produit L'espace Urbain?: les Exemples de Yaoundé (Cameroun) et D'Antananarivo (Madagascar)', *Afrique contemporaine*, No. 217, pp. 217-229.

This paper is based on a study carried on street children in Yaoundé (Cameroon) and Antananarivo (Madagascar), and shows that while street children are becoming more and more visible the authorities seem largely unaware of this phenomenon, Meanwhile, NGOs are increasingly interested and investing social policy issues related to street children. This leads the author to ask under what values and what standards are the NGOs acting and how their activities engage with larger government plans for urban policies.

## 302. Moyer, Eileen

2004, 'Popular Cartographies: Youthful Imaginings of the Global in the Streets of Dar es Salaam, Tanzania', *City & Society*, Vol. 16. Issue 2, pp. 117–143.

Data for this paper was gathered during 1999-2000 research among a group of poor urban youth struggling to make a living in the streets of the downtown business district of Dares Salaam. This location allows for an exploration of various themes related to labor, power, and the politics of development. This article attempts to unravel some of the complex relationships between contemporary processes of globalization and young peoples' efforts to make meaningful lives for themselves. The author looks at the various socioeconomic activities that youth have in the streets through creative endeavors that earn them a non-consistent but useful income.

## 303. Moyer, Eileen

2006, 'Not Quite the Comforts of Home: Searching for Locality Among Street Youth in Dar es Salaam', In *Crisis and Creativity: Exploring the Wealth of the African*, ed Piet Konings and Dick Foeken, Leiden: Brill, pp. 163-196.

This chapter examines two 'locations' that formed important loci among those young men and women living and working in the streets of Dar es Salaam with whom the author worked in Dar es Salaam, the first tied to work and the second to leisure and relaxation. It examines how these locales factor into the imaginaries of the young people who inhabit them, as well as into the imaginaries of more established residents of the city, focusing on contestation and social unease. The author shows how uprooted from their childhood homes and often isolated from rural support networks, these urban dwellers work to develop networks that provide safety and security from the threats of street life, protection from police harassment and, importantly, friendship and love.

## 304. Murphy, William P.

2003, 'Military Patrimonialism and Child Soldier Clientalism in the Liberian and Sierra Leonean Civil Wars', *African Studies Review*, Vol. 46, no. 2, pp. 61-87.

This article uses a Weberian model of patrimonialism to analyse clientalist and 'staff' roles of child soldiers in the military regimes of the civil wars in Liberia and Sierra Leone. It thereby examines institutional aspects of child soldier identity and behaviour not addressed in other standard models of child soldiers as coerced victims, revolutionary idealists, or delinquent opportunists. It shifts analytical attention from nation-State patrimonialism to the patrimonial dimensions of rebel regimes. It locates child soldiers within a social organization of domination and reciprocity based on violence structured through patronage ties with military commanders and identifies child soldier 'staff' functions within the administration of a patrimonial regime.

## 305. Nolte, Insa

2004, 'Identity and Violence: the Politics of Youth in Ijebu-Remo, Nigeria', *The Journal of Modern African Studies*, Vol. 42, no. 1, pp. 61-89.

Focusing on youth conflicts in Sagamu, the capital of Ijebu-Remo in the Yoruba-speaking southwest of Nigeria, this article examines the politics of youth in this city, from the 1950s to the present. The author discusses the emergence of the politics of youth in the 1950s and 1960s, how it drew on pre-colonial discourse and was closely associated with the emergence of Remo's anti-federal postcolonial political identity. Since Nigeria's political and economic decline in the mid-1980s, strong feelings of exclusion- strengthened further by the political sidelining of Yoruba-speaking politicians in national politics between 1993 and 1999 - have contributed to an increase of nationalist sentiment in Remo youth politics. Apart from archival and library research, the article is based on fieldwork and interviews carried out in Remo and Ogun State between 1996 and 2002.

## 306. Olubanke, Akintunde Dorcas

2008, 'The Role of the Church in the Care of Street Children in Africa', *African Journal of Biblical Studies*, Vol. 26, no. 2, pp. 25-36.
ASC Subject Headings: Africa; street children; Church.

This paper first discusses the causes of this phenomenon, including social causes, economic woes, political instability and broken families. Next, it explores what can be done about the problem by the Church, suggesting that the Church should intensify its teaching on sexual abstinence and marriage principles, and should provide a refuge for street children, where they can sleep, have meals and can be schooled. Worthy of emulation by the Church in Africa are the activities of WATOTO, an offshoot of the Pentecostal Church of Uganda.

## 307. Ondimu, Kennedy Nyabuti

2007, 'Workplace Violence Among Domestic Workers in Urban Households in Kenya: a Case of Nairobi City', *Eastern Africa Social Science Research Review*, Vol. 23, no. 1, pp. 37-61.

This paper discusses findings of a study conducted in 2004/2005 on the prevalence and impact of domestic labour migration in Nairobi, Kenya. Specifically, the paper examines the profile of domestic workers and the extent of their vulnerability and exposure to different forms of abuse. The study integrated both qualitative and quantitative research techniques to attain its objectives. The qualitative approach included a key informant survey and in-depth interviews. The quantitative approach involved a cross-sectional household stratified sample survey in urban residential areas in Nairobi. The results reveal that, overall, children account for a higher proportion of domestic workers, most of them girls from poor families.

## 308. Panzer, Michael G.

2009, 'The pedagogy of Revolution: Youth, Generational Conflict, and Education in the Development of Mozambican Nationalism and the State, 1962-1970', *Journal of Southern African Studies*, Vol. 35, no 4, pp. 803-820.

This article addresses a lacuna in analyses of FRELIMO's nationalist development during the 1960s and illustrates how African nationalist groups, operating within another nation's sovereign space, could build legitimacy and establish hegemony. Specifically, the article examines the impact of generational tensions between Mozambican youth and FRELIMO party 'elders' that emerged at the FRELIMO Mozambique Institute secondary school in Dar es Salaam, Tanzania, in the second half of the 1960s, at a particularly critical moment in FRELIMO's anticolonial war against Portugal.

## 309. Pype, Katrien

2007, 'Fighting Boys, Strong Men and Gorillas: Notes on the Imagination of Masculinities in Kinshasa', *Africa: Journal of the International African Institute*, Vol. 77, no. 2, pp. 250-271.

This article provides Insight into the current violent practices of urban youngsters in Kinshasa, Democratic Republic of Congo (DRC). At nightfall youth gangs transform the streets of Kinshasa's townships into arenas of the fight. Frequent regular clashes between these gangs create young violent leaders, who not only sow terror but also provide security for the inhabitants (young and old) of their territories. Although many of these boys and young men are trained in foreign fighting styles such as judo, jujitsu and karate, in the public clashes between the fighting groups, these boys and young men perform 'mukumbusu'. This fighting style, inspired and based on the gorilla, was invented during the last decade of colonialism, and is an original mixture of a traditional Mongo wrestling practice, 'libanda', and Asian and Western fighting practices. In the article, the author scrutinizes the practices of these young fighters through the diverse images of masculinity ('kimobali') upon which they draw, such as the fighter and the soldier; and the models of masculinity that they contest, the sapeur and the staffeur.

## 310. Richards, Paul

2005, 'To Fight or to Farm?: Agrarian Dimensions of the Mano River Conflicts (Liberia and Sierra Leone)', *African Affairs*, Vol. 104, no. 417, pp. 571-590.

This study argues that while wars in Liberia and Sierra Leone have been linked to the condition of urbanized Youth, recent research in southeastern Sierra Leone and northwestern Liberia suggests the rural context is of greater significance. The fighting was mainly in rural areas, involved mainly rural youth, and adapted itself to their local concerns. A model of war as the work of urban criminal gangs reflecting local student politics in the 1970s and embraced internationally, is ripe for replacement by a model of war as agrarian revolt. The key to conflict resolution in the region, it is suggested, is an emphasis on agrarian justice, including reform of customary land and marriage law.

## 311. Richter, Linda M.

2006, 'In-Migration and Living Conditions of Young Adolescents in Greater Johannesburg, South Africa', *Social Dynamics*, Vol. 32, no. 1, pp. 195-216.

This article compares the access to services, housing and household amenities, and family characteristics of children born in the Greater Johannesburg metropolis with those of in-migrant children. The article also examines other indicators of child well-being related to parental care and schooling. In-migrant children, particularly children who have lived previously in rural areas and/or have recently migrated into the city, are significantly disadvantaged in comparison to long-term resident children in terms of parental education and occupation, housing type and ownership, access to electricity, refuse removal, water and sanitation. The article is based on a Children's School Survey conducted in 2002.

## 312. Richter, Linda M.

2009, 'Adolescents in the City: Material and Social Living Conditions in Johannesburg-Soweto, South Africa', *Urban Forum*, Vol. 20, no. 3, pp. 319-334.

This paper describes the material and social living conditions of 5,367 young adolescents in Johannesburg-Soweto, South Africa, in 2002-2003. The majority of children in South Africa's urban hub have adequate access to basic services. However, social conditions are a key concern - lack of financial support by parents; defaulting caregiver roles to grandparents; minimal or no contact with fathers; and poor school performance. Weakened levels of family support in urban environments may negatively impact on adolescent development. In the long term, family systems as well as other social networks and institutions need to be strengthened to improve adolescent outcomes.

### 313. Samara, Tony Roshan

2005, 'Youth, Crime and Urban Renewal in the Western Cape', *Journal of Southern African Studies*, Vol. 31, no. 1, pp. 209-227.

This study examines the politics of urban renewal in Cape Town's Central Business District, paying particular attention to efforts to control the presence of street children in the central city. The author argues that the attention given to street children and the negative impact they are said to have on urban renewal constitutes a moral panic driven by and contributing to a vision of development that leaves relatively untouched the inequalities of apartheid. The author's contention is that criminalization of street children raises serious doubts as to how well new progressive approaches to both crime reduction and development will survive urban renewal efforts that many feel reproduce the city's division into developed and underdeveloped areas.

### 314. Sanni, Amidu

2007, 'The Nigerian Muslim Youth and the Shari'a Controversy: Issues in Violence Engineering in the Public Sphere', *Journal of Oriental and African Studies*, Vol. 16, pp. 119-133.

This paper investigates the impulses behind the growing controversy surrounding the introduction of Sharia and the participation of you and concludes that violence as an ideology in the public sphere has far-reaching implications for development and social cohesion, especially in developing countries with strong confessional differences. Violence, the author argues, has become a new medium of expression in the pursuit of this cause since the 1970s, but has assumed a more systematic and ideological character since the return to democratic rule in 1999.

### 315. Sanni, Amidu

2008, 'Terror in the name of God and the Society: the Nigerian Youth and the Economy of Violence', *Journal of Oriental and African Studies*, Vol. 17, pp. 87-102.

This paper argues that a culture of denial or marginalization has largely been responsible for the tradition of violence, which militant and radical elements in religious and ethnic circles have often employed in their

190

systemic campaigns. It concludes by saying that a proper appreciation of the real causes of violence by the State and a genuine commitment to their solution through dialogue and interactive means remains the viable option in the enthronement of world peace and order.

### 316. Shorr, Lindsy

2007, 'The Post-Conflict Treatment of Child Soldiers: the Case of Liberia', *East African Journal of Peace & Human Rights*, Vol. 13, no. 1, pp. 1-29.

This article takes issue with the universalism that surrounds definitions and responses to child soldiers, arguing that they neither deter the use of children in conflict nor provide appropriate post-conflict reintegration of child soldiers. The article provides a critical pluralist approach to the post-conflict treatment of child soldiers. In particular, the discussion focuses on the potential options for handling former Liberian child combatants who fought in the Liberian civil war. The case of Liberia poses an opportunity to institutionalize the first active juvenile chamber for the prosecution and rehabilitation of former child soldiers. Such a chamber, modelled after the framework set forth by former United Nations Secretary-General Kofi Annan in response to Sierra Leone, would incorporate principles of Disarmament, Demobilization and Reintegration (DDR) to encourage both domestic political transition and a changed understanding of what is a child soldier and what constitutes their appropriate post-conflict treatment.

### 317. Singh, Divya

2007, 'When a Child is not a Child: the Scourge of Child Soldiering in Africa', *African Human Rights Law Journal*, Vol. 7, no. 1, pp. 206-224.

This article examines the reasons why any country and/or military group/person would introduce children to armed conflict and the effect of such engagement on the child victim: physical danger, psychological trauma and educational stultification. The use of child soldiers has been expressly prohibited by various international treaties under international human rights law, humanitarian law, criminal law and even labour law. The consequences of child soldiering for Africa must impact, directly, on the growth, development and regeneration programmes earmarked for the upliftment of the continent, on the ability of Africa to take its place as a player in the global arena, and on the promotion of the human rights ethos underpinning the African renaissance. A priori, all States have a fundamental responsibility to end the use of child soldiers in Africa. To this end, the author makes recommendations for the elimination of the practice, at both national and international levels.

## 318. Stohl, Rachel J.

2002, 'Under the Gun: Children and Small Arms', *African Security Review*, Vol. 11, no. 3, pp. 17-25.

This paper highlights the plight of children on the African continent that have suffered immensely from the proliferation and misuse of small arms, including death, injury, displacement, separation from families, loss of access to health, humanitarian and educational services, and lack of economic opportunities. Further, it shows that over 300,000 children serve as child soldiers, relying on small arms as their tools of war. The author argues that while the international community has worked to establish protections for children for over 50 years, children continue to suffer, and hopes that the recent UN Special Session on Children adopted 'A world fit for children', will begin to seriously address a comprehensive approach to eliminating the negative impacts of small arms proliferation on children in conflict.

## 319. Stovel, Laura

2008, "There's no Bad Bush to Throw Away a Bad Child': 'Tradition'-Inspired Reintegration in Post-War Sierra Leone', *The Journal of Modern African Studies*, Vol. 46, no. 2, pp. 305-324.

This research draws on interviews with diverse Sierra Leoneans to examine the assumptions behind the communitarian ideal captured in the phrase 'there is no bad bush to throw away a bad child' often stated in reference to rehabilitating ex-combatant youth. Government and civil society leaders in African transitional States often use rituals and expressions inspired by tradition to facilitate the integration of ex-combatants and displaced people. In Sierra Leone, this expression conveys a vision of African society as inherently forgiving and inclusive, and of Africans as needing to be amongst their own people. This ideal was perfectly suited for the needs of an impoverished State seeking to ease the strain on cities, and relying on communities' organic capacities to absorb their own people. The author argues that while 'There is no bad bush' promotes a form of reconciliation defined as peaceful coexistence, it lacks the elements of justice required for deep reconciliation to occur.

### 320. Straker, Jay

2007, 'Youth, Globalisation, and Millennial Reflection in a Guinean Forest town', *The Journal of Modern African Studies*. Vol. 45, no. 1, pp. 299-319.

This article argues for broadening the research agenda of African youth studies, calling for increased attention to the interpretive work performed by provincial youths as they try to understand and hopefully alter the future prospects of their communities in the new century. Examining a questionnaire administered in the spring of 2000, in which local high-school students commented on multifaceted changes unfolding around them in the forest administrative capital of N'Zérékoré, the author shows how ideas about the meanings of globalization and 'the millennium', intertwined with experiences of a recent refugee 'crisis', are shaping Guinean youths' sociopolitical reflections and yearnings. In doing so, he stresses just how complicated and cosmopolitan 'provincial' life, particularly for young people, has become in Guinea's forest region, as well as the variety and sophistication of the historical 'materials' and interpretive schemes through which these youths depict and judge possible local futures.

### 321. Ukeje, Charles

2001, 'Youths, Violence and the Collapse of Public Order in the Niger Delta of Nigeria', *Africa Development*, Vol. 26, no. 1/2, pp. 337-366.

The primary focus of this paper is on the role of youths in the violent conflicts plaguing the Niger Delta oil region of Nigeria since the early 1990s, when the Ogonis embarked on a mass protest against an alliance between the Nigerian State and foreign oil companies, especially Shell Petroleum Development Company. The author discusses the causes and dimensions of violent conflicts in the Niger Delta, the reasons for youth involvement in grassroots politics and violence in the area, the security implications and the reactions of government and the multinational oil companies.

## 322. Van Blerk, Lorraine

2006, 'Diversity and Difference in the Everyday Lives of Ugandan Street Children: the Significance of Age and Gender for Understanding the Use of Space', *Social Dynamics*, Vol. 32, no. 1, pp. 47-74.

Drawing on a range of children-centred qualitative methods, this article focuses on street children's use of urban space in Kampala, Uganda. The article demonstrates the importance of considering variables such as gender and age in the analysis of street children's sociospatial experiences which, to date, have rarely been considered in other accounts of street children's lives. In addition, the article highlights the need for also including street children's individuality and agency into understanding their use of space. The article concludes by arguing for policies to be sensitive to the diversity that characterizes street children's lives and calls for a more nuanced approach where policies are designed to accommodate street children's age and gender differences, and their individual needs, interests and abilities.

## 323. Waller, Richard

2006, 'Rebellious Youth in Colonial Africa', *The Journal of African History*, Vol. 47, no. 1, pp. 77-92.

This article surveys the issue of rebellious youth that alarmed colonial authorities as an introduction to the two studies that follow in this issue of 'The Journal of African History'. It considers both the creation of images of youthful defiance as part of a debate about youth conducted largely by their seniors and the real predicaments faced by young people themselves. The author argues that concern revolved around the meanings of maturity in a changing world where models of responsible male and female adulthood, gendered expectations and future prospects were all in flux. The article concludes by suggesting a number of areas, including leisure and politics, where the voice of youth might be more clearly heard, and proposes comparisons – with the past, between racial groups and between 'town' and 'country' – that link the varied experiences of the young in Africa.

## 324. Wesonga, Pamela W., Joshua J. Akong'a, and Richard O. Musebe

2005, 'Constraints Facing Youth Groups in their Endeavour to Reduce Poverty in Mathare Slum, Nairobi', *Mila*, Vol. 6, pp. 51-63.

Based on research among the poor urban youth in Mathare slum in Nairobi, Kenya, this paper looks at the role of youth groups in restoring the personal and social identity of these young people. Particularly, it focuses on the constraints these youth groups are facing in handling youth problems. The paper shows that youth groups face economic problems such as unemployment, lack of finance, equipment and facilities; social problems such as lack of formal education and housing; political problems emanating from the provincial administration, the police and youth group leaders; and environmental problems such as sanitary facilities. The paper also discusses coping strategies developed by youth as well as suggestions for improving the effectiveness of youth groups, addressing agencies such as the government, NGOs, churches, the community and youth group leaders and members.

# Online Useful Sources (Selected)

## Bibliography

Cheney, Kristen, 2012, 'Africa', in Oxford Bibliographies Online, ed., Heather Montgomery. New York: Oxford University Press. Available at http://oxfordbibliographiesonline.com/page/childhood-studies

CODESRIA DOCUMENTATION AND INFORMATION CENTRE, 2011, 'Children's Agency and Development in African Societies: Bibliography' available at http://codesria.org/IMG/pdf/Bibliography_CODESRIA_Child_Youth_Studies_Institute_2011.pdf

## Online Sources

Africa Access (http://www.africaaccessreview.org/aar/index.html)

African Studies Center at Leiden (http://www.ascleiden.nl/Library/Abstracts/ASA-Online/AllIssues.aspx)

Aluka (http://www.aluka.org/)

Childhood in Africa (http://www.afrchild.ohio.edu/CAJ/)

CODESRIA Documentation and Information Centre (CODICE) online catalogue (http://codice.codesria.sn:81/)

Five College Archives Digital Access Project (http://clio.fivecolleges.edu/)

Google Scholar (http://scholar.google.com/)

WorldCat (http://www.worldcat.org/)

www.ingramcontent.com/pod-product-compliance
Lightning Source LLC
Chambersburg PA
CBHW050651280326
41932CB00015B/2862